The Romantic Tradition in American Literature

The Romantic Tradition in American Literature

Advisory Editor

HAROLD BLOOM
Professor of English, Yale University

THE

BIRD AND THE BELL,

WITH

OTHER POEMS

BY

CHRISTOPHER PEARSE CRANCH

ARNO PRESS

A NEW YORK TIMES COMPANY

New York • 1972

Reprint Edition 1972 by Arno Press Inc.

Reprinted from a copy in The University
of Illinois Library

The Romantic Tradition in American Literature
ISBN for complete set: 0-405-04620-0
See last pages of this volume for titles.

Manufactured in the United States of America

৩ঌ৩ঌ৩ঌ৩ঌ৩ঌ৩ঌ৩ঌ

Library of Congress Cataloging in Publication Data

Cranch, Christopher Pearse, 1813-1892.
    The bird and the bell, with other poems.

    (The Romantic tradition in American literature)
    I. Title. II. Series.
PS1449.C8B5 1972   811'.3   72-4960
ISBN 0-405-04632-4

THE

BIRD AND THE BELL,

WITH

OTHER POEMS.

BY

CHRISTOPHER PEARSE CRANCH.

BOSTON:

JAMES R. OSGOOD AND COMPANY,

LATE TICKNOR & FIELDS, AND FIELDS, OSGOOD, & CO.

1875.

12 13 35

UNIVERSITY PRESS: WELCH, BIGELOW, & CO.,
CAMBRIDGE.

As one who in some cellar crypt has kept
His wines of many an autumn vintage, pressed
From wildwood grapes, or vineyard fields that slept
On sunny hillsides, by his own hand dressed;
And calls his neighbors in to taste and share
His store; yet overvaluing, perchance,
What seemed to keep for him a flavor rare
Which love might prize when critics frown askance:
So to my board I bid my friends, and ope
The hoarded flasks of many a varying year, —
The verse from lonely dells of dreamland won,
Or by sweet toiling on the sun-flecked slope
Of life, ere yet my summer leaves were sere
In lengthening shadows of the sinking sun.

CONTENTS.

SONNETS.

POEMS OF THE WAR.

THE BIRD AND THE BELL,

WITH

OTHER POEMS.

THE reader will find in this poem allusions to events which have passed in Italy, — fluent when the lines were written, but now crystallized into history, — and prophecies, some of which have come, or are coming true, while others have been fulfilled otherwise than was foreboded. These passages of the poem may therefore lose somewhat of the flavor they might have had if read at that period. The rapid and wonderful scene-shifting, too, that has gone on in the great European theatre of Church and State may have the effect of dimming their freshness somewhat. But the thoughts and principles here embodied can never cease to interest all who care for liberty of thought and speech, and will maintain a supreme importance so long as the Romish Church holds to its assumptions in the face of the nineteenth century.

If much of the language in these verses apostrophizing this mighty organization seems too unqualified and denunciatory, it will be seen that I have endeavored to give praise also where I felt it to be due. But the poem was written in Catholic Europe, where I was daily impressed with characteristics which stood out more baldly prominent than any which come to our notice in America.

THE BIRD AND THE BELL

I.

'T WAS earliest morning in the early spring,
In Florence.   Winter, dark and damp and chill,
Had yielded to the fruit-trees' blossoming,
Though sullen rains swept from the mountains still.
The tender green scarce seemed to have a will
To peep above the sod and greet the sky, —
Like an o'er-timid child who dreads a stranger's eye.

II.

The city slumbered in the dawning day ; —
Old towers and domes and roof-tiles looming dim,
Bridges and narrow streets and cloisters gray,
And sculptured churches, where the Latin hymn
By lamplight called to mass.   As o'er a limb
The spells of witchcraft strong but noiseless fall,
The shadows of the Past reigned silent over all.

III.

Waking from sleep, I heard, but knew not where,
A bird, that sang alone its early song.
The quick, clear warble leaping through the air, —
The voice of spring, that all the winter long
Had slept, — now burst in melodies as strong
And tremulous as Love's first pure delight ; —
I could not choose but bless a song so warm and bright.

IV.

Sweet bird ! the fresh, clear sprinkle of thy voice
Came quickening all the springs of trust and love.
What heart could hear such joy, and not rejoice ?
Thou blithe remembrancer of field and grove,
Dropping thy fairy flute-notes from above,
Fresh message from the Beauty Infinite
That clasps the world around and fills it with delight !

V.

It bore me to the breeze-swept banks of bloom,
To trees and falling waters, and the rush
Of south-winds sifting through the pine-grove's gloom ;
Home-gardens filled with roses, and the gush
Of insect-trills in grass and roadside bush ;
And apple-orchards flushed with blossoms sweet ;
And all that makes the round of nature most complete.

VI.

It sang of freedom, dimmed by no alloy;
Peace, unpossessed upon our troubled sphere;
Some long Arcadian day of love and joy,
Unsoiled by fogs of superstitious fear;
A world of noble beings born to cheer
The wilderness of life, and prove the fact
Of human grandeur in each thought and word and act.

VII.

What was it jarred the vision and the spell,
And brought the reflux of the day and place?
Athwart the bird's song clanged a brazen bell.
Nature's improvisations could not face
That domineering voice; and in the race
Of rival tongues the Bell outrang the Bird, —
The swinging, clamoring brass which all the city heard.

VIII.

Santa Maria Novella's Church, hard by,
Calling its worshippers to morning prayer,
From its old *Campanile* lifted high
In the dull dampness of the clouded air,
Poured out its monotones, and did not spare
Its ringing shocks of unremitting sound,
That soon my warbler's notes were swept away and drowned.

IX.

Down from the time-stained belfry clanged the bell,
Joined in a moment by a hundred more.
Had I not heard the bird, I might have well
Floated on that sonorous flood that bore
Away all living voices, as with roar
Of deep vibrations, grand, monastic, bold,
Through street and stately square the metal music rolled.

X.

Oft have I listened in the dead of night,
When all those towers like chanting priests have prayed;
And the weird tones seemed tangled in the height
Of palaces, — as though all Florence made
One great ghost-organ, and the pipes that played
Were the dark channelled streets, pouring along
In beats and muffled swells the deep resounding song.

XI.

So now the incessant peal filled all the air,
And the sweet bird-voice, utterly forced away,
Ceased.   And it seemed as if some spirit fair
Were hurled into oblivion; and the day
Grew suddenly more darkly, grimly gray,
Like a vast mort-cloth stretched from south to north,
While that tyrannic voice still rang its mandates forth.

XII.

And so I mused upon the things that were,
And those that should be, or that might have been;
And felt a life and freedom in the air,
And in the sprouting of the early green,
I could not match with man, who builds his screen
Darkening the sun, and in his own light stands,
And casts the shadow of himself along the lands.

XIII.

For him who haunts the temples of the Past,
And shapes his fond ideals by its rules;
Whose creed, whose labors, are but thoughts recast
In worn and shrunken moulds of antique schools, —
Copies of copies, wrought with others' tools;
For whom law stands for justice, Church for God,
Symbol for fact, for right divine the tyrant's rod; —

XIV.

Who fears to utter what his reason bids,
Unless it wears the colors of a sect;
Who hardly dares to lift his heavy lids,
And greet the coming Day with head erect,
But apes each general posture and defect
Entailed by time, — alert in others' tracks,
Like owls that build in some time-mantled ruin's cracks; —

XV.

For him yon clanging Bell a symbol bears,
That deadens every natural voice of spring.
Fitter for him the croaking chant, the prayers,
The torch, the cross, the censer's golden swing,
The organ-fugue, — a prisoned eagle's wing
Beating the frescoed dome, — the empty feast
Where at his tinselled altar stands the gay-robed priest.

XVI.

O mighty Church ! who, old, but still adorned
With jewels of thy youth, — a wrinkled bride
Affianced to the blind, — so long hast scorned
The rising of the inevitable tide
That swells and surges up against thy pride, —
Thou, less the artist's than the tyrant's nurse,
Blight of philosophy, false star of poet's verse ! —

XVII.

What though thy forms be picturesque and old,
And, clustered round thee, works of noblest art
Hallow thy temples !   Once they may have told
Profound emotions of the inmost heart;
Now shadowed by a faith that stands apart,
And scowls against the sunlight shared abroad,
Burning in altar-nooks its candles to its god !

XVIII.

The saints who toiled to help the world's distress ;
The noble lords of thought and speech divine ;
The prophets crying through Time's wilderness ;
The vast discoveries, the inventions fine
That stamped upon the centuries a sign
Of grandeur, — all, like music thundered down
By stern cathedral bells, were silenced by thy frown.

XIX.

Chained to Madonnas and ascetic saints,
Even Art itself felt thy all-narrowing force.
The painter saw thee peeping o'er his paints ;
The sculptor's thought was fettered from its source ;
Thy gloomy cloisters shaped the builder's course ;
Thy organ drowned the shepherd's festive flute
With penitential groans, as though God's love were mute.

XX.

And yet, because there lurked some element
Of truth within the doctrine, — to man's need
Some fitness in the form ; since more was meant
And more expressed than in the accepted creed, —
The artist's genius giving far less heed
To formulas than to his own ideal, —
The hand and heart wrought works the world has stamped
                as real.

XXI.

What didst thou for the already teeming soil
Of souls like Dante, Raphael, Angelo,
Save to suggest a theme or pay their toil ?
While they o'erlooked their prison walls, and so
Caught from the skies above and earth below
Splendors wherewith they lit thy tarnished crown,
And clothed thee with a robe thou claimest as thine own.

XXII.

Names that in any age would have been great,
Works that to all time speak, and so belong,
Claim not as thine ; nor subsidize the fate
That gave them to the nations for a long,
Unceasing heritage.   Amid a throng
Of starry lights they live.   Thy clanging bells
Can never drown their song, nor break their mighty spells.

XXIII.

No mother thou of Genius, but the nurse.
Seek not to stamp a vulgar name upon
The sons of Morning.   Take the Poet's verse,
But not the Poet.   He is not thy son.
Enough for thee, if sometimes he hath gone
Into thy narrow fold from pastures wide,
Where through immortal flowers God pours the living tide.

XXIV.

Enough if he hath decked thee with the wealth
Of his heaven-nurtured spirit, — showering gems
Of thought and fancy, coining youth and health
To gild with fame thy papal diadems ;
Plucking life's roses with their roots and stems
To wreathe an altar which returned him naught
But the poor patronage of some suspected thought.

XXV.

What didst thou for the studious sage who saw
Through nature's veils the great organic force, —
Who sought and found the all-pervading law
That holds the rolling planets in their course ?
When didst thou fail to check the flowing source
Of truths whose waters needs must inundate
The theologic dikes that guarded thy estate ?

XXVI.

Is there a daring thought thou hast not crushed ?
Is there a generous faith thou hast not cursed ?
Is there a whisper, howe'er low and hushed,
Breathed for the future, but thou wast the first
To silence with thy tortures, — thou the worst
Of antichrists, and cunningest of foes
That ever against God and man's great progress rose ?

1 *

XXVII.

Yet life was in thee once.   Thy earlier youth
Was flushed with blossoms of a heavenly bloom.
Thy blight began, when o'er God's common truth
And man's nobility thou didst assume
The dread prerogative of life and doom;
And creeds which served as swaddling-bands were bound
Like grave-clothes round the limbs laid living underground.

XXVIII.

When man grows wiser than his creed allows,
And nobler than the church he has outgrown;
When that which was his old familiar house
No longer is a home, but all alone,
Alone with God, he dares to lift the stone
From off the skylight between heaven and him, —
Then shines a grander day, then fade the spectres grim.

XXIX.

And never yet was growth, save when it broke
The letter of the dead scholastic form.
The bark drops off, and leaves the expanding oak
To stretch his giant arms through sun and storm.
The idols that upon his breast lay warm
The sage throws down, and breaks their hallowed shrine,
And follows the great hand that points to light divine.

XXX.

But thou, O Church! didst steal the mother's mask,
The counterfeit of Heaven, — so to enfold
Thy flock around thee.   None looked near, to ask
" Art thou our mother, truly ? "   None so bold
As lift thy veils, and show how hard and cold
Those eyes of tyranny, that mouth of guile,
That low and narrow brow, the witchcraft of that smile, —

XXXI.

That subtle smile, deluding while it warmed ;
That arrogant, inquisitorial nod ;
That hand that stabbed, like Herod, the new-formed
And childlike life which drew its breath from God,
And, for that star by which the Magi trod
The road to Bethlehem, the Good Shepherd's home,
Lit lurid idol-fires on thy seven hills of Rome.

XXXII.

Rome, paralyzed and dumb, — who sat a queen
Among the nations, now thy abject slave ;
Yet muttering in her cell, where gaunt and lean
Thy priests have kept her pining !   Who shall save
And lift the captive from her living grave ?
Is there no justice left to avert her doom,
Where monarchs sit and play their chess-games on her
        tomb ?

XXXIII.

And thou, too, Venice, moaning by the sea,
Which moans and chafes with thee, on Lido's beach, —
Thou, almost in despair lest there should be
In Europe's life no life within thy reach,
No respite from thy tyrant, — thou shalt teach
Thy Austrian despot yet what hoarded hate
And sudden strength can do to change thy sad estate!

XXXIV.

For, lo, the fires are kindled.   Hark! afar,
At last the thunders mutter under ground,
The northern lights flash cimeters of war,
Sardinia's trumpets to the battle sound.
See Florence, Parma, Modena, unbound,
Leap to their feet, — and stout Romagna brave
The Cardinal's frown, and swear to cower no more a slave!

XXXV.

See Sicily, whose blood is Ætna's veins
Of sleepless fire, heave with volcanic pants,
Seething, a restless surge of hearts and brains,
Till Garibaldi's quick Ithuriel lance
Wakes the whole South from its long, troubled trance,
And Naples, catching the contagious flame,
Welcomes her hero in with blessings on his name!

XXXVI.

The nations that in darkness sat have seen
The light.   The blind receive their sight again.
The querulous old man who stands between
His children and their hopes, with threats insane,
Trembles, as though an earthquake split in twain
The crumbling rock beneath Saint Peter's dome ;
And the last hiding-place of tyranny — is Rome.

XXXVII.

For Italy, long pining, sad, and crushed,
Has hurled her royal despots from the land.
Back to her wasted heart the blood has gushed.
Her wan cheek blooms, and her once nerveless hand
Guides with firm touch the purpose she has planned.
Thank God ! thank generous France ! the battle smoke
Lifts from her bloody fields.   See, at her feet her yoke !

XXXVIII.

Not like a maddened anarch does she rise :
The torch she holds is no destroying flame,
But a clear beacon, — like her own clear eyes
Straining across the war-clouds ; and the shame
Of wild misrule has never stained her name.
Calm and determined, politic yet bold,
She comes to take her place, — the Italy of old.

XXXIX.

She asks no boon, except to stand enrolled
Among the nations.   Give her space and air,
Our Sister.   She has pined in dungeons cold.
A little sunshine for our Sister fair,
A little hope to cover past despair.
God's blessing on the long-lost, the unbound !
The earth has waited long ; the heavens now answer —
      " Found ! "

XL.

The nations greet her as some lovely guest
Arriving late, where friends pour out the wine.
Ay, press around, and pledge her in the best
Your table yields, and in her praise combine !
And ye who love her most, press near, and twine
Her locks with wreaths, and in her large dark eyes
See all her sorrowing past, and her great future rise !

XLI.

But thou who claim'st the keys of God's own heaven,
And who wouldst fain usurp the keys of earth, —
Thou, leagued with priests and tyrants who have given
Their hands, and pledged their oaths to blight the birth
Of thine own children's rights, — for scorn and mirth
One day shalt stand, thy juggling falsehoods named,
Thy plots and wiles unmasked, thy heaven-high titles
      shamed !

XLII.

Look to the proud tiara on thy brow !
Its gems shall crush thee down like leaden weights.
Thy alchemy is dead ; and wouldst thou now
Thunder anathemas against the states
Whose powers are Time's irrefragable fates ?
Look to thy glories ! they must shrink away, —
With meaner pomp must fall, and sink into decay.

XLIII.

Lo, thou art numbered with the things that were,
Soon to be laid upon the dusty shelves
Of antiquaries, — once so strong and fair,
Now classed with spells of magic, midnight elves,
And all half-lies, that pass away themselves
When once a people rises to the light
Of primal truths and comprehends its heaven-born right.

XLIV.

Toil on ; but little canst thou do to-day.
The sun is risen.   The daylight dims thy shrines.
The age outstrips thee, marching on its way,
And overflowing all thy boundary lines.
How art thou fallen, O star !   How lurid shines
Thy taper underneath the glowing sky !
How feeble grows thy voice, how lustreless thine eye !

XLV.

Like some huge shell left by the ebbing tide,
  In which once dwelt some wonder of the sea,
Thou liest, and men know not that thy pride
  Of plaee outlives thy earlier potency,
  But, coming nearer to thy mystery,
  Might call thee lovely, did not thy decay
And death-like odor drive them in contempt away.

XLVI.

So perish like thee all lies stereotyped
  By human power or devilish artifice, —
Dark blot on Christ's pure shield, soon to be wiped
  Away, and leave it fair for Heaven's free kiss ;
  So perish like thee, drowned in Time's abyss,
  All that hath robbed strong Genius of its youth,
All that hath ever barred the struggling soul from truth !

XLVII.

And yet we need not boast our larger scope
  In this broad land, if creeds of later stamp
Still cast their gloom o'er manhood's dearest hope,
  Still quench the heavenward flame of Reason's lamp,
  And dogmas shamed by science still can cramp
  The aspiring soul in dungeons scarce less drear
Than those of older times, when faith was one with fear.

XLVIII.

Nor dream that here the inquisitorial chair
Is but a byword, though we flush and weep
In honest indignation, when we hear
Chains clank in Rome, and wonder how the cheap
And common truth of Heaven must cringe, and creep,
And mask its face, lest Mother Church disown
The rebel thought that flouts the apostolic throne !

XLIX.

If we indeed are sure our faith is best,
Then may we dare to leave it large and free,
Nor fear to bring the creed to reason's test;
For best is strongest, fearing not to see
As well as feel.   Then welcome, Liberty !
Down with the scaffolding the priest demands !
Let Truth stand free, alone, a house not built with hands!

L.

Down with the useless and the rotting props
That only cumber and deface each wall !
Off with the antiquated cloth that drops
Moth-eaten draperies round the columns tall.
Nor needs the heavenly Architect our small
Superfluous tricks of ornament and gilt,
To deck the royal courts his wisdom planned and built,

B

LI.

He wills a temple beautiful and wide
As man and nature, — not a cloister dim,
Nor strange pagoda of barbaric pride
Scrawled o'er with hieroglyph and picture grim
Of saint and fiend.   Why seek to honor him
By crusting o'er with gold of Palestine
The simple, stainless dome whose builder is divine?

LII.

Thanks to the Central Good, the inflowing Power,
The Primal Life in which we live and move, —
The aroma of the soul, the passion-flower
We bear upon our hearts, the deathless love
Of right, outlives device, and floats above
All human creeds, though armed with power to brave
The scholar's daring thought, and make the world their
——— slave.

LIII.

The music of the soul can ne'er be mute.
What though the brazen clang of antique form
Stop for a hundred years the angel's lute,
The angel smiles, and when the deafening storm
Has pealed along the ages, with the warm
Touch the immortals own, he sings again,
Clearer and sweeter, like the sunshine after rain.

LIV.

He sings the song no tyrant long resists;
He sings the song the world perforce must join,
Though ages stand as notes.　For he insists
With such sweet emphasis, such chords divine,
That, soon or late, along the living line
Of hearts that form Humanity, there thrills
A sympathetic nerve no time or custom kills.

LV.

Humanity must answer when God speaks,
As sure as echo to the human voice.
And every grand o'ertopping lie which breaks
With furious flood and century-deafening noise
In the eternal symphony that joys
Along, is but some baser pipe or chord
That shall be tuned again when Reason sits as lord.

LVI.

Eternal Truth shines on o'er Error's cloud,
Which, for a little, veils the living light.
Therefore, though the true bard may sing aloud
His soul-song in the unreceptive night,
His words — swift, arrowy fires — must fly and light,
Sooner or later, kindling south and north,
Till skulking Falsehood from her den be hunted forth.

LVII.

Work on, O fainting hearts! Through storm and drouth,
Somewhere your wingéd heart-seeds will be blown,
And plant a living grove ; — from mouth to mouth,
O'er oceans, into speech and lands unknown,
Even till the long-foreseen result be grown
To ripeness, filled like fruit with other seed,
Which Time shall sow anew, and reap when men shall need.

LVIII.

There is no death, but only change on change.
The life-force of all forms, in tree and flower,
In rocks and rivers, and in clouds that range
Through heaven, in grazing beasts, and in the power
Of mind, goes forth forever, an unspent dower,
Glowing and flashing through the universe,
Kindling the light of stars, and joy of poet's verse !

LIX.

Each hour and second is the marriage-morn
Of spirit-life and matter ; as when kings
Wed peasants, and their simple charms adorn
With Oriental gems and sparkling rings
And diadems, and with all royal things
Making their eyes familiar, — so, with tones
Sweet and unheard before, conduct them to their thrones.

LX.

One mighty circle God in heaven hath set,
Woven of myriad links, — lives, deaths unknown, —
Where all beginnings and all ends are met
To follow and serve each other, — Nature's zone
And zodiac, round whose seamless arc are strewn
A million and a million hues of light
That blend and glow and burn, beyond our realm of night.

LXI.

O ye who pined in dungeons for the sake
Of truths which tyrants shadowed with their hate;
Whose only crime was that ye were awake
Too soon, or that your brothers slept too late, —
Mountainous minds ! upon whose tops the great
Sunrise of knowledge came, long ere its glance
Fell on the foggy swamps of fear and ignorance, —

LXII.

The time shall come when from your heights serene
Beyond the dark, ye will look back and smile
To see the sterile earth all growing green,
Where Science, Art, and Love repeat Heaven's style
In crowded city and on desert isle,
Till Eden blooms where martyr-fires have burned,
And to the Lord of Life all hearts and minds are turned.

LXIII.

The seeds are planted, and the spring is near.
Ages of blight are but a fleeting frost.
Truth circles into truth.   Each mote is dear
To God.   No drop of ocean e'er is lost,
No leaf forever dry and tempest-tossed.
Life centres deathless underneath decay,
And no true word or deed can ever pass away.

LXIV.

And ye, O Seraphs in the morn of time !
Birds whose entrancing voices in the spring
Of primal Truth and Beauty, were the chime
Of heaven and earth ! still we may hear you sing.
No clang of hierarchal bells shall ring,
To drown your carol, in the airs that move
And stir the dawning age of Liberty and Love !

LXV.

Light, — light breaks on the century's farthest round ;
Light in the sky, light in the humblest home.
The unebbing tides of God, where errors drowned
Sink down to fathomless destruction, come
Swelling amain.   Truth builds her eternal dome
Vast as the sky.   Nations are linked in one.
Light, Love, henceforth shall reign forever and alone !

THE THREE MUSES.

In a deep vale enclosed by mountains steep,
A still, green sheltered nook hid far away,
Where grand old forest-trees in shadowy sleep
Nodded above a stream that all the day
Ran rippling down o'er sun-flecked rocks and stones,
And filled the air with murmuring undertones;
Where from the sky the golden sun of June
Shed softened radiance through the stillest noon;
And in the verdure of the oaks that spread
Their gnarled and mossy branches overhead,
The shy thrush trilled his liquid clarionet
Minute by minute, with his soul all set
To music in each gush of peerless tone,
While with a bubbling base the brook played on; —
Deep in that vale so dreamy, still, and cool,
A youth lay tranced, till visionary things
Seemed real, and his heart was over-full
Of thoughts and fancies and imaginings.

And as he mused beside the flowing stream,
There came to him what seemed a waking dream.
Three radiant forms he saw before him stand, —
Three woodland nymphs, perchance, he thought, — who met
His wondering gaze, each with a beckoning hand,
While he, abashed, bewildered, stood.   And yet —
For so our dreams will mix our memories dim —
Not all unknown their faces seemed to him.
And he was bound, as by a spell, to choose
One of the three to be his guiding muse.

So stood they beckoning, and yet stood apart,
As if a separate purpose each impelled ;
While a divided worship in his heart
In doubtful poise his soul and senses held.

" Strange, — it was so in Ida's vale," he mused,
" The shepherd-prince, abashed, perplexed, confused,
Stood in the presence of the radiant Three,
To choose the goddess of his destiny.
So shone upon his soul like dawning skies
The electric splendor of Olympian eyes.
Somehow I seem to know these forms of light.
Somewhere they have lit my pathway, day and night.
If through this veil of dreams I could but hear

Their voices, my bewildered sense would clear.
And yet, alas ! I cannot give to each,
While thus to me their wooing arms they reach,
The pledge of homage and fidelity,
The golden apple Nature gave to me."

Then one of them drew near.   She held a lyre,
And with low strains the enchanted silence broke.
Her mystic tones diffused a subtle fire,
And in his soul sweet harmonies awoke.
Then in his hands she placed a golden lute,
And bade him touch its sympathetic chords.
No longer now he stood abashed and mute;
But sang a prelude soft in simple words, —
A lay of love and longing, — till his song
Grew deeper, richer, blending with the strings;
Then soaring as on swift expanded wings,
With gathered strength it ran through varying moods,
And echoed from the rocks and rang around the woods.

Then said the muse, " 'T is thus that I will dower
The soul that feels my all-pervading power.
This nest of wingéd harmonies shall give
Responses to each mood that he hath known,
And all the subtler shades of feeling live

2

Perfected life, when wed to chord and tone.
And thou shalt know how tone embodies love,
As speech embodies thought, and haply reach
The large, creative power of those who move
The heart by music, superseding speech.
And thus would I enroll thee in the bands
Who dedicated youth and age to me
In costly strains that speak to all the lands
The language of the gods.   Look up and see ! "

The youth looked up, and on the mountain height
He saw a group of forms enwreathed with light;
While floated down such strains as never ear
Had dreamed of in our dim, discordant sphere.

Filled with the rapturous symphony
That from that orchestra divine
Came flowing like a spiritual wine
Into his soul, the youth in ecstasy,
As when a flower is bowed with morning dews,
Bent low before the muse.

" Spirit of Harmony divine," he said,
" Ah, worshipped from my boyhood's early hour !
How oft, how long my footsteps have been led
Apart from men, by thy mysterious power !

How oft the deep enchanted waves of tone
Have lured me with a rapture all too sweet!
Thine were those tides, O fairest, thine alone,
That from the dull shore swept my willing feet.
Though my untutored hands but feebly ring
The imperfect chords, the themes I may not sing,
Yet fain would I thy humble votary be,
And find my muse, my guiding star, in thee!"

But now a touch, as 't were some earthly maiden,
Dissolved the trance with which his soul was laden.
Before him stood the second of the three;
And on his ear these accents rang in free
And healthy measure, like the morning air.
"Dream not," she said, "these vague, seductive dreams.
I give thee choice of forms and colors rare, —
Fair images of skies, of trees, of streams;
All shapes of beauty and all forms of power;
The themes that through the past and present shine;
The varying lights that flash from hour to hour; —
Life, Nature, Spirit. Be the effort thine;
The out-world wooes thee. Give thy utmost heart
To enrich the ever-growing realm of Art.
Be this thy love, thy toil, thy high ambition,
To tread the path of Raphael, Claude, and Titian.

Here choose thy brothers, who in robes of light
Throng the green shades beneath yon woody height ! ''

He looked, and saw a train as bright as those
Who just had vanished, grouped in grand repose :
Great, earnest brows, and loving, piercing eyes
Which saw the unveiled divinity that lies
In forms and faces and in trees and skies.
And as they passed, woods, rocks, and mountains took
A richer light and color.   Then the brook
More silvery ran, the sky shone deeper blue,
The clouds were tinted with an opal hue.
The landscape glowed as if it gave its heart
To those who loved it through the soul of art.
" Go forth," the goddess said.   " The earth is fair.
Where beauty smiles, the artist's work is there.
What nobler task than this, canst thou but stay
The fleeting splendors of a single day ! ''

Thus while with breezy tones she spoke,
The youth stood rapt and listening.
The artist-fire, long smouldering, woke ;
And with a sudden spring
He seized his paints and pencils eagerly,
And bent before the muse a lowly knee.

" Alas ! and was I blind ? " he said, " and thou,
The charm of earth and air, wast here e'en now ?
Thou, with all color and rare forms allied, —
One with all nature, — thou wast by my side !
And could I slight the presence that illumes
The eye-beams and the splendors of the world, —
The mists of dawn, the depths of forest glooms,
The crimson clouds in western twilights furled,
The river, and the mountain, and the face
Of man and maid, and childhood's winning grace ?
Have I not known, O queen, O muse of art,
Thy service, — all the joyous toil of those
Who give the flowering of their hope and heart —
A sweet and yet so oft a thorn-clad rose —
To thee, as kneeling now I dare to touch
Thy garment's hem — "

     E'en then he felt approach
The third bright form.   Taller and fairer she
Than the other two.   A queenlier majesty
Upon her brow.   Around her all the air
Seemed touched with wandering odors sweet and rare,
Wafted from unseen nooks of eglantine.
She neither smiled nor frowned.   She made no sign,
But only stood before him.   Every grace
Of mingled earth and heaven illumed her face

And shaped her form.   Upon her brow a star
Flamed, like the diamond planet of the dawn
When night's cold coronets are all withdrawn
And scattered through her solitudes afar, —
Flamed and streamed backward through her golden hair ;
And all the freshness of the summer morn
Breathed from her presence.   Fairest of the fair
She stood, of all in bright Olympus born.

She spoke.   But hardly had she moved her lips,
When in a gradual, yet not dark eclipse
Her sisters faded.   Rather did it seem
Those muses three had mingled into one, —
One form to whom all beauty tribute paid,
One bringer of an overpowering dream,
One central light all other lights obeyed.
And all that he had dreamed and felt and known,
And all that he could hear, imagine, see,
Flushed in the Morning Star of Poesy.
She was a presence that did well comprise
The soul and essence of all other art ;
For all the world contains of sweetest, lies
Like an aroma hoarded in her heart.
Now *all* seemed music, *all* was magic hue,
All was unfettered joy and inspiration.

Now Beauty bathed the universe anew,
And kindled thought, and fired imagination.
Then rose the strong necessity to write,
As once to sing, to paint his fondest dream.
Flooded he stood as in the auroral light,
Or in the waves of some great flowing stream ;
While that one voice again and yet again
Came, earnest as a cry of joy or pain.
It called upon him as a trumpet calls
The laggard soldier to his spear and shield.
It seemed to sweep him as a leaf that falls
Whirls in the autumn blast across the field.
It pressed upon him as the truth sublime
Lay on the prophets of the olden time, —
The soul within the soul, the hidden life,
The fount of dreams, the vision and the strife
Of thoughts that seized on every other force,
And turned it to their own resistless course.

For the muse spake with words that came
Leaping into his heart like flame : —

    " Why should I show to thee here
    Shadows of poet and seer,

Bards of the olden time,
Singers of lofty rhyme ?
Beauty and truth are the same
Now as of old, and the flame
Of the morning on Homer's brow
Is a flame of the morning now.
The poets sit ever apart,
With heaven and earth in their heart, —
One truth, and unnumbered hints ;
One light, and a thousand tints ;
Ages of speech and of tone,
One mystical voice alone.

" When the bard utters his own,
Rivals and peers there are none.
His life is the life of the All.

   His dreams are of air and of fire ;
To the depths of all nature they call

   In the thirst of their soaring desire.
And ever by day and by night
The arrows of thought's delight,
Feathered with musical words,

   Barbed with the adamant truth,
Fly gentle and swift as the winging of birds

   To the bosom of beauty and youth."

And still she spoke; and still he listened there,
And felt the ambrosial breathing fan his hair;
And still his soul rose brimming to her eyes,
As swells the sea beneath the moonlit skies.

" Foremost of seers and strong creators he
Who steeps life, nature, heaven, in poesy.
He is no athlete trained to win a prize
In an arena thronged with vulgar eyes;
No juggler with his tricks of tinselled phrase,
Cheap bubbles blown to catch ephemeral praise.
No lawless passion and no trivial aim
Shall dim his vision clear, or damp his flame.
Strong be his faith, and pure as it is strong,
The heart-throb pulsing through the poet's song.
'T is his to read the sunshine and the storms,
The mystic alphabet of natural forms,
The deeper lore of dreams and heart and brain,
The heights, the depths, the glory and the pain.

" The muse who leads the poet guides the spheres.
One orbit serves for both.   He cannot stoop
To palter to unsympathetic ears.

   His wings must never droop.
Buoyed by a wind that blows beyond the stars,
Lit by a sun that never fades or sets,

He comes to proffer through fate's prison-bars
   The soul's strong amulets.
To press the wine of life from bitter hours ;
To open doors where morning never streamed ;
To find in common fields that rarest flowers
   Are nearer than we dreamed ;
To intone the music of the deepest heart
Through all the changing chords of joy and pain, —
Where canst thou track a loftier flight of Art ?
   Where seek diviner gain ? "

She ceased, yet seemed to speak.   The youth
Still heard that voice of love and truth ;
And all his soul stood over-flushed,
And every clamorous impulse hushed.

Then, reverent, before her face
He half upraised his downcast eyes,
His heart all glowing in the light and grace
That matched her radiance with the unsaddened skies.
" Thou Presence dear and great ! " he cried ;
" Thou wast the earliest at my side.
Thou on the topmost golden stair of art
With thrilling voice dost stand and call to me.
O fairest goddess, I must give my heart,
My spirit, and my life to none but thee ! "

THE SHADOWED RIVER.

DEDICATED TO THE MEMORY OF A. J. DOWNING.

In the clear September moonlight
 Dark the eastern mountains rise,
And the river calm as ever
 One broad lake of silver lies.

Like a frame, the leafy garden
 Clasps the dreamy picture round,
And I gaze for hours upon it,
 By the spell of beauty bound.

O'er the water's burnished mirror
 Darkly glide the shadowed ships;
So the glowing past is shaded
 By our sorrowing thoughts' eclipse.

Bright, broad River! flow forever
 In the moonlight to the sea;

But those joyous days thou never,
  Never canst bring back to me.

See, the frame the leafy garden
  Arches round the pictured scene,
Like a cypress wreath is growing
  Dark, — too dark for this, I ween.

He who wreathed the lovely landscape
  With these green and shady bowers,
Taken from us, went forever
  With his fleeting garden flowers.

And the lawn beneath the linden,
  And the shrubs and vines so green,
And the fragrant beds of roses,
  And the winding paths between,

And the house in beauty bowered,
  Rare in beauty of its own,
Ne'er again may hear the music
  Of those days forever flown ;

Ne'er again shall hear the laughter
  Of the joyous company
Whom the festal days of summer
  Crowned with mirth and melody.

Silent River, sadly flowing !
    Shadowed sails like thoughts of pain
Slowly cross thy gleaming silver,
    But they catch the light again.

Darkly bend the mountains o'er thee,
    Dim and dusky in the night,
But their summits woo the moonbeams,
    And are touched with heavenly light.

Life is rich, and nature lavish ;
    Providence is large as Fate :
Many a joy they hide in secret
    For the lone and desolate.

After sunset clouds of crimson ;
    After twilight comes the moon ;
After moon-set still the starlight ;
    Still the morning's daily boon.

And the cloud that lowers the darkest
    Holds the blessing of the rain ;
And the grief that stuns the deepest
    Hath another touch than pain.

NEWBURGH ON THE HUDSON, September, 1852.

NOVEMBER TREES.

LET poets sing of their leafy trees
   When the tides of summer fancies swell
And rock their thoughts, as a tropic breeze
   Rocks the bee in a lily's bell ;
But give me a harp whose ring is sharp,
   Tuned for November melodies,
That I may roam the bleak hills alone
   And sing of the gray and leafless trees.

Their boughs are bare in the twilight dark,
   Cold and bare when the moon is high,
Like the cordage and masts of a stranded bark
   That warp and freeze in a polar sky.
There is never a leaf the sky-born thief
   Did not hurry away ere its color was gone.
But the boughs, though bare, to me are as fair
   As the naked forms of the Parthenon.

Where the branches part in the dusky wood
　　The golden mist of the sunset streams ;
And tracts of starlit solitude
　　Glimmer at night on a world of dreams.
The wind is chill on the rugged hill,
　　And the early snow is gathering ;
But the winter is naught, for the boughs are fraught
　　With the flow of sap and the hope of spring.

O patriots whom the tyrant's hate
　　O'ershadows like the winter drear,
While like the patient trees ye wait,
　　Freedom, the nation's spring, is near.
Never despair, though the darkening air
　　Sweep all your summer leaves away ;
The wind may rifle your branches bare,
　　Your leaves will burst anew in May !

　　　1852.

THE FLOWER AND THE BEE.

LOVE me as the flower loves the bee.
Ask no monopoly of sympathy.
    I must flit by,
Nor stay to heave too deep a sigh,
Nor dive too deep into thy charms.
Untwine thy prisoning arms;
    Let the truth-garnering bee
    Pass ever free!

Yield all the thymy fragrance I can draw
    From out thy soul's rich sweetness.   Not forever
Can lovers see one truth, obey one law,
    Though they spend long endeavor.
Give me thy blossoming heart;
I can but take thereof that part
    Which grand Economy
    Permitteth me to see.

Friendship and love may last in name,
   As lamps outlive their flame ;
An earthly tie may bind our hands ;
   The spirit snaps the bands.
If Nature made us different,
Our compliments in vain are spent ;
But if alike, ah, then I rest in thee
As in the flower's full heart the sated bee.

   1852.

THE CATARACT ISLE.

I WANDERED through the ancient wood
　That crowns the cataract isle.
I heard the roaring of the flood
　And saw its wild, fierce smile.

Through tall tree-tops the sunshine flecked
　The huge trunks and the ground,
And the pomp of fullest summer decked
　The island all around.

And winding paths led all along
　Where friends and lovers strayed,
And voices rose with laugh and song
　From sheltered nooks of shade.

Through opening forest vistas whirled
　The rapids' foamy flash,
As they boiled along and plunged and swirled,
　And neared the last long dash.

I crept to the island's outer verge,
   Where the grand, broad river fell, —
Fell sheer down mid foam and surge
   In a white and blinding hell.

The steady rainbow gayly shone
   Above the precipice,
And the deep low tone of a thunder groan
   Rolled up from the drear abyss.

And all the day sprang up the spray
   Where the broad white sheets were poured,
And fell around in showery play,
   Or upward curled and soared.

And all the night those sheets of white
   Gleamed through the spectral mist,
When o'er the isle the broad moonlight
   The wintry foam-flakes kissed.

Mirrored within my dreamy thought,
   I see it, feel it all, —
That island with sweet visions fraught,
   That awful waterfall.

With sunflecked trees, and birds and flowers,
   The Isle of Life is fair;
But one deep voice thrills through its hours,
   One spectral form is there, —

A power no mortal can resist,
   Rolling forever on, —
A floating cloud, a shadowy mist,
   Eternal undertone.

And through the sunny vistas gleam
   The fate, the solemn smile.
Life is Niagara's rushing stream;
   Its dreams — that peaceful isle!

September, 1853.

IN THE GARDEN.

WITH rose and orange scents this place was laden;
  The summer air was quivering thick with birds.
In these cool garden walks I met the maiden
  Whose beauty robs her praisers' tongues of words.

A crimson rose was in her hand.   She held it
  Close to my lips, — in truth, a flower divine;
But I looked in her eyes and scarcely smelled it,
  But took the flower and hand in both of mine.

These are the shades where arm in arm for hours
  We walked, — brief hours of throbbing pain and bliss.
Here drank love's bitter-sweet, deep hid in flowers;
  Here gave and took our last despairing kiss.

And where is she, the fair light-footed comer?
  I pace these lonely garden walks in vain.
O long-lost joy! O Rose of love and summer!
  That day ye bloomed will never come again!

IN THE PINE WOODS.

DIM distances that open through the pines,
   Blue misty mountains sleeping in the west :
Beneath the tall tree-trunks I watch your lines
   Waving beyond the field's unshadowed breast.

Amid the pine-tops sighs the wandering air,
   The locust's trill swells dying on the breeze,
The cloudless August noon to me doth wear
   The sadness of life's distant melodies.

Between me and the far horizon stream
   The viewless spirits of the days long gone.
I see the landscape as from out a dream ;
   I hear the wind's sigh — as if 't were my own.

LUNA THROUGH A LORGNETTE.

I TO-NIGHT was at a party
Given by the fair Astarte.
Star-like eyes danced twinkling round me;
Cold they left me, as they found me.
One bright vision, one face only,
Made me happy and yet lonely.
It was hers to whom is given
Rule by night, — the queen of heaven.
" Ah, how fair she is ! " I muttered,
Like a night-moth as I fluttered
Round her light, but dared not enter
That intensely radiant centre,
Whence she filled the clouds about her,
Whence she lit the very outer
Darkness, and the ocean hoary
With her floods of golden glory.

Some one, then, as I stood gazing,
Filled too full of her for praising,

Of the old time vaguely dreaming,
When she took a mortal seeming;
When the shepherd sprang to meet her,
And he felt a kiss, ah, sweeter
Than e'er lips of mortal maiden
Gave her lover passion-laden, —
Some one with a sneer ascetic
Broke in on my dream poetic.
" I see more," he said, " than you, sir;
Would you like a nearer view, sir ? "
And with that, politely handing
A lorgnette, he left me standing,
In her face directly gazing;
And I saw a sight amazing.
Ah, these dreadful magnifiers
Kill the life of our desires.
Shall I tell you what I saw then ?
All of you around me draw then.

Can she be as once I thought her, —
Phœbus' sister, Jove's fair daughter?
Whom the night-flowers turn to gaze on,
Whom the sleeping streams emblazon:
Lover's planet, lamp of heaven,
Goddess to whom power is given

Over tides and rolling oceans,
Over all the heart's emotions!

Ah, farewell, my boyish fancies!
Farewell, all my young romances!
As that orb that shone Elysian
On my young poetic vision,
As that crescent boat which lightly
Tilted o'er the cloud-rack nightly,
I again can see her never,
Though I use my best endeavor.
On me once her charms she sprinkled,
Now her face is old and wrinkled.
As Diana chaste and tender,
Can I now as once defend her?
She is full of histories olden
Wrapped up in her bosom golden.
Sorceress of strange beguiling,
Thousands perished by her smiling, —
Girls kept waking, old men saddened,
Lovers lost, and poets maddened.
Now the well-armed eye of Science
Bids her magic spells defiance;
Moonstruck brains by moonlight haunted
Telescopes have disenchanted.

Talk not of the brow of Dian.
Gentle bards, you may rely on
What I 've seen to-night ; 't is clearly
Known the moon 's constructed queerly,
Full of wrinkles, warts, and freckles,
Gilded cracks and spots and speckles ;
As if in wandering through the void,
Her face were marked with varioloid.
Then her cheeks and eyes so hollow,
That I 'm sure the bright Apollo
Ne'er would know her for his sister,
Nor Endymion have kissed her.

Nay, good Moon, I 'm loath to slander
Thy mysterious beauty yonder ;
Rather as I gaze upon thee,
Truer lines be written on thee.
Take away your telescope, sir ;
Let me still, as ever, hope, sir.
Ill does it become a lover
All the bare truth to discover.
Reach me, friends, a brimming beaker ;
Wine shall make my vision weaker.
Songs of olden days come sing me,
Charms that cheat the senses bring me.

Nay, I have a sweet suspicion
It was a distorted vision.
What I saw that looked so queerly,
Was exaggeration merely.
Things remote by law of nature
Should be kept within their stature.
Telescopic eyes are clever
Things to own; but use them never!

So, fair Moon, again I 'm dreaming
On thy face above me beaming!
Orb of beauty, mid star-clusters
Hanging heavy with thy lustres;
Saturated with the sun-fire,
Which thou turnest into moon-fire,
Raying from thy fields and mountains,
Silvering earth's rejoicing fountains,
Crystal vase with light o'er-brimming;
Eye of night with love-tears swimming;
Heaven's left heart, in music beating
Through the cloud robes round thee fleeting;
Cheering all within, without thee,
Even the wind-chased mists about thee, —
Though I mocked thy face mysterious,
I have grown more sage and serious.

Cold astronomers may show thee
Rough in feature, fair I know thee !
At thy critics thou art laughing,
Spite of all their photographing,
In their rigid prose detailing
Every spot and every failing.
I will be thy enamored poet,
Though my friends may smile to know it ;
For my dreams do scorn alliance
With these prying thieves of science.

IN THE PALAIS ROYAL GARDEN.

IN the Palais Royal Garden I stood listening to-day,
Just at sunset, in the crowd that flaunted up and down
     so gay
As the strains of " Casta Diva " rose and fell and died
     away.

Lonely in the crowd of French I stood and listened to
     the strain,
And the breath of happier hours came blowing from the
     past again;
But the music brought a pleasure that was near akin to
     pain.

Italy, dear Italy, came back, with all her orange flowers,
With her sapphire skies and ocean, with her shrines and
     crumbling towers,
And her dark-eyed women sitting under their vine-shaded
     bowers.

And the rich and brilliant concerts in my own far distant
      land,
Where the world-renownéd singers, circled by the orchestral
      band
Poured their music on the crowds like costly wine upon
      the sand.

All the aroma of the best and brightest hours of love and
      song
Mingled with the yearning music, floated to me o'er the
      throng.
But it died as died the sunset.   Ah, it could not linger
      long!

Through the streets the carriages are rolling with a heavy
      jar,
Feebly o'er the staring gas-lamps glimmers here and there
      a star.
Night looks down through narrow spaces; men are near,
      the skies are far.

Far too are my friends, the cherished, — north and south
      and o'er the sea.
And to-night I pant for music and for life that cannot be,
For the foreign city's crowd is naught but solitude to me.

    PARIS, August, 1854.

CORNUCOPIA.

THERE 's a lodger lives on the first floor ;
   (My lodgings are up in the garret ;)
At night and at morn he taketh a horn,
   And calleth his neighbors to share it, —
A horn so long and a horn so strong,
   I wonder how they can bear it.

I don't mean to say that he drinks, —
   I might be indicted for scandal.
But every one knows it, he night and day blows it,
   (I wish he 'd blow out like a candle !)
His horn is so long, and he blows it so strong,
   He would make Handel fly off the handle.

By taking a horn I don't hint
   That he swigs either rum, gin, or whiskey.

It 's we, I am thinking, condemned to be drinking
   His strains that attempt to be frisky,
But are grievously sad.   A donkey, I add,
   Is as musical, braying in *his* key.

It 's a puzzle to know what he 's at.
   I could pity him if it were madness.
I never yet knew him to play a tune through ;
   And it gives me more anger than sadness
To hear his horn stutter and stammer in utter
   Confusion of musical badness.

At his wide-open window he stands,
   Overlooking his bit of a garden.
One can see the great ass at one end of his brass
   Blaring out, never asking your pardon.
Our nerves though he shatter, to him it 's no matter,
   As long as his tympanums harden.

He thinks, I 've no doubt, it is sweet, —
   While time, tune, and breath are all straying.
The little house-sparrows feel all through their marrows
   The jar and the fuss of his playing ;
The windows are shaking, the babies are waking,
   The very dogs howling and baying.

One note out of twenty he hits ;
　　Blows all his *pianos* like *fortes*.
His time is his own.　He goes sounding alone,
　　A sort of Columbus or Cortes,
On a perilous ocean, without any notion
　　Whereabouts in the dim deep his port is.

If he gets to his haven at last,
　　He must needs be a desperate swimmer.
He has plenty of wind, but no compass, I find ;
　　And being a veteran trimmer,
He veers and he tacks, and returns on his tracks ;
　　And his prospects grow dimmer and dimmer.

Like a man late from club, he has lost
　　His key, and around stumbles, moping,
Touching this, trying that, — now a sharp, now a flat, —
　　Till he strikes on the note he is hoping ;
And a terrible blare at the end of his air
　　Shows he 's got through at last with his groping.

There, he 's finished, — at least for a while ;
　　He is tired, or come to his senses ;
And out of his horn shakes the drops that were borne
　　By the winds of his musical frenzies.

3 *

There's a rest, thank our stars! of ninety-nine bars,
    Ere the tempest of sound recommences.

When all the bad players are sent
    Where all the false notes are protested,
I'm sure that Old Nick will there play him a trick,
    When his bad trump and he are arrested;
And down in the regions of discord's mad legions
    His head with two French horns be crested!

PARIS, August, 1856.

A FRIEND.

A FRIEND! it seems a simple boon to crave,
    An easy thing to have;
Yet our world differs somewhat from the days
    Of the romancer's lays.
A friend? why, *all* are friends in Christian lands.
    We smile and clasp the hands
With merry fellows o'er cigars and wine;
    We breakfast, walk, and dine
With social men and women. Yes, we are friends;
    And there the music ends!
No close heart-heats, — a cool, sweet ice-cream feast;
    Mild thaws, to say the least;
The faint slant smile of winter afternoons;
    The inconstant moods of moons
Sometimes too late, sometimes too early rising,
    But for a night sufficing;

Showing a half-face, clouded, shy, and null ;
  Once in a month at full ;
Lending to-night what from the sun they borrow ;
  Quenched in his light to-morrow.
If thou 'rt my friend, show me the life that sleeps.
  Down in thy spirit's deeps ;
Give all thy heart, the thought within thy thought.
  Nay, I 've already caught
Its meaning in thine eyes, thy tones. What need
  Of words ? Flowers keep their seed.
I love thee ere thou tellest me " I love."
  We both are raised above
The ball-room puppets with their one-typed faces,
  Chatting stale commonplaces,
Or aiming to express a lifeless thought
  In tinselled phrase, worth naught ;
Or, at the best, throwing a passing spark
  Like fireflies in the dark, —
Not the continuous lamplight of the soul,
  Which, though the seasons roll
Without, on tides of ever-varying winds,
  The watcher never finds
Flickering in draughts, or dim for lack of oil.
  There is a clime, a soil

Where loves spring up twin-stemmed from mere chance
        seed
      Dropped by a word, a deed.
As travellers toiling through the Alpine snow
      See Italy below;
Down glacier slopes and craggy cliffs and pines
      Descend upon the vines,
And meet the welcoming South who half-way up
      Lifts her o'erbrimming cup, —
So, blest is he, from peaks of human ice
      Lit on this paradise;
Who mid the jar of tongues hears music sweet;
      Who in some foreign street
Thronged with cold eyes, catches a hand, a glance
      That deifies his chance, —
That turns the dreary city to a home,
      The blank hotel to a dome
Of splendor, while the unsympathizing crowd
      Seems with his light endowed.
Many there be who call themselves our friends;
      Yet ah ! if Heaven but sends
One, only one, so mated to our soul,
      To make our half a whole,
Rich beyond price are we.   The millionnaire
      Without such boon is bare,

Bare to the skin, — a gilded tavern-sign
    Creaking with fitful whine
Beneath chill winds, with none to look at him
    Save as a label grim
To the good cheer and company within
    His comfortable inn.

THE AUTUMN RAIN.

I.

ROOF and spire and darkened vane
Steep and soak in the night-long rain
That drips through the barns on the golden grain ;
And a drowning mist sweeps over the plain,
And spatters with mud the rutted lane
And the dead flower-stalks that bud not again.

II.

Wind-driven drops of the autumn rain,
Beat, beat on the window-pane !
Beat, beat, sorrowful rain !
Drive through the night o'er the desolate plain !
Beat and sob to the old refrain,
And weep for the years that come not again.

III.

Years, with your mingling of joy and of pain, —
Joys long forgotten, and cares that remain ;
Hopes lying stranded and choked in the drain
Of the down-rushing river of fate, — I would fain
Sigh with the night-wind and weep with the rain,
For ye come not again ! — ye come not again !

1855.

SPIRITS IN PRISON.

O YE who, prisoned in these festive rooms,
  Lean at the windows for a breath of air,
Staring upon the darkness that o'erglooms
  The heavens, and waiting for the stars to bare
Their glittering glories veiled all night in cloud, —
  I know ye scorn the gas-lights and the feast.
I saw you leave the music and the crowd,
  And turn unto the casements opening east.
I heard you sigh, " When will the dawn's dull ashes
  Kindle their fires behind yon fir-fringed height ?
When will the prophet clouds with golden flashes
  Unroll their mystic scrolls of crimson light ? "
Fain would I come and sit beside you here,
  And, silent, press your hands, and with you lean
Into the night-air, mingling hope and fear
  With vain regrets for days that might have been.

E

Are we not brothers?　In the throng that fills
　　These strange, enchanted rooms, we met.　One look
Told that we knew each other.　Sudden thrills,
　　As of two lovers reading the same book,
Ran through our hurried grasp.　But when we turned,
　　The scene around was smitten with a change;
The lamps with lurid torchlight flared and burned:
　　And　through　the　wreaths　and　flowers — O mockery
　　　　strange! —
The prison walls with ghastly horror frowned.
　　Scarce hidden by vine-leaves and clusters thick,
A grim, cold iron grating closed around.
　　Then from our silken couches leaping quick,
We hurried past the dancers and the sights,
　　Nor heeded the entrancing music then,
Nor the fair women scattering soft delights
　　In flower-like flush of dress, nor paused till when,
Leaning against our prison-bars, we gazed
　　Into the dark, and wondered where we were.
Speak to me, brothers! for ye stand amazed.
　　I come — your secret burden here to share.

I know not this mysterious land around,
　　Nor what those shapes may be that loom obscure.

Odors of gardens and of woods profound
    Blow in from out the darkness, fresh and pure.
Faint sounds of friendly voices come and go,
    That seem to lure us forth into the air.
But whence they come perchance no ear may know,
    And where they go perchance no foot may dare !

A realm of shadowy forms out yonder lies;
    Beauty and Power, fair dreams pursued by Fate,
Wheel in unceasing vortex, and the skies
    Flash with strange lights that bear no name or date.
Sweet winds are breathing that just fan the hair,
    And fitful gusts that howl against our bars,
And harp-like songs, and groans of wild despair,
    And angry clouds that chase the trembling stars.
And on the iron grating the hot cheek
    We press, and forth into the night we call,
And thrust our arms, that, manacled and weak,
    Clutch but the empty air, and powerless fall.

And yet, O brothers, we who cannot share
    This life of lies, this stifling day in night,
Know we not well that if we did but dare
    Break from our cell, and trust our manhood's might,
When once our feet should venture on these wilds,
    The night would prove a still sweet solitude,

Not dark for eyes that, earnest as a child's,
　　Strove in the chaos but for truth and good ?
And O, sweet liberty — though wizard gleams
　　And elfin shapes should frighten or allure —
To find the pathway of our hopes and dreams;
　　By toil to sweeten what we might endure;
To journey on, though but a little way,
　　Towards the morning and the fir-clad heights;
To follow the sweet voices, till the day
　　Bloomed in its flush of colors and of lights;
To look back on the valley and the prison,
　　These windows smouldering still with midnight fires,
And know the joy and triumph to have risen
　　Out of that falsehood into new desires !
O friends ! it may be hard our chains to burst,
　　To scale the ramparts, pass the sentinels.
Dark is the night; but we are not the first
　　Who break from the enchanter's evil spells.
Though they pursue us with their scoffs, their darts,
　　Though they allure us with their siren song,
Trust we alone the Light within our hearts.
　　Forth to the air!　Freedom will dawn erelong !

Paris, 1858.

BLONDEL.

AT the castle's outer door
Stood Blondel the Troubadour.
Up the marble stairs the crowd,
Pressing, talked and laughed aloud.
Upward with the throng he went;
With a heart of discontent
Tuned his sullen instrument,
Tried to sing of mirth and jest
As the knights around him pressed;
But across his heart a pang
Struck him wordless ere he sang.

Then the guests and vassals roared,
Sitting round the oaken board :
" If thou canst not wake our mirth,
Touch some softer rhyme of earth.
Sing of knights in ladies' bowers,
Twine a lay of love and flowers ! "

" Can I sing of love ? " he said,
And a moment bowed his head ;
Then looked upward, out of space,
With a strange light in his face.

Said Blondel the Troubadour,
" When I hear the battle roar,
And the trumpet tones of war,
Can I tinkle my guitar ? "

" But the war is o'er," said all ;
" Silent now the bugle's call,
Love should be the warrior's dream,
Love alone the minstrel's theme.
Sing us *Rose-Leaves on a Stream*."

Said Blondel : " Not rose-leaves now ;
Leafless thorns befit the brow.
In this crowd my voice is weak,
But ye force me now to speak.
Know ye not King Richard groans
Chained 'neath Austria's dungeon stones ?
What care I to sing of aught
Save what presses on my thought ?
Over laughter, song, and shout
From these windows swelling out,

Over passion's tender words
Intonating through the chords,
Rings the prisoned monarch's lay
Through and through me night and day.
And the only strain I know
Haunts my brain where'er I go,
Trumpet tones that ring and ring
Till I see my Richard king.

" Gallants, hear my song of love,
Deeper tones than courtiers move.
Hear my royal captain's sigh, —
England, Home, and Liberty ! "

Then he struck his lute and sang
Till the shields and lances rang :
How for Christ and Holy Land
Fought the Lion Heart and Hand ;
How the craft of Leopold
Trapped him in a castle old ;
How one balmy morn in May,
Singing to beguile the day
In his tower, the minstrel heard
Every note and every word ;
How he answered back the song,

" Let thy hope, my king, be strong;
We will bring thee help erelong ! "

Still he sang, " Who goes with me ?
Who is it wills King Richard free ?
He who bravely toils and dares,
Pain and danger with me shares;
He whose heart is true and warm,
Though the night perplex with storm
Forest, plain, and dark morass,
Hanging rock and mountain pass,
And the thunder bursts ablaze, —
He is the lover that I praise ! "

As the minstrel left the hall,
Silent, sorrowing, sat they all.
Well they knew his banner sign,
The Lion Heart of Palestine.
Like a flame the song had swept
O'er them.   Then the warriors leapt
Up from the feast with one accord,
Pledged around their knightly word.
From the old castle's windows rang
The last verse the minstrel sang,
Then from out the castle door
They followed the brave Troubadour.

THE OLD DAYS AND THE NEW

I.

A POET came singing along the vale:
    " Ah, well-a-day for the dear old days!
They come no more as they did of yore,
    By the flowing River of Aise."

He piped through the meadow, he sang through the grove:
    "Ah, well-a-day for the good old days!
They have all gone by, and I sit and sigh
    By the flowing River of Aise.

" Knights and ladies, and shields and swords, —
    Ah, well-a-day for the grand old days!
Castles and moats, and the bright steel coats,
    By the flowing River of Aise.

4

" The lances are shivered, the helmets rust ;
  Ah, well-a-day for the stern old days !
And the clarion's blast has rung its last
  By the flowing River of Aise.

" For the warriors who swept to glory and death, —
  Ah, well-a-day for the brave old days ! —
They have fought and have gone, and I sit here alone
  By the flowing River of Aise.

" The queens of beauty whose smile was life, —
  Ah, well-a-day for the rare old days ! —
With love and despair in their golden hair,
  By the flowing River of Aise,

" They have flitted away from hall and bower ;
  Ah, well-a-day for the rich old days !
Like the sun they shone, like the sun they have gone,
  By the flowing River of Aise.

" And buried beneath the pall of the past, —
  Ah, well-a-day for the proud old days ! —
Lie valor and worth, and the beauty of earth,
  By the flowing River of Aise.

" And I sit and sigh by the idle stream ;
   Ah, well-a-day for the bright old days ! —
For naught remains for the poet's strains
   But the flowing River of Aise."

II.

Then a voice sang out from the oak overhead :
   " Why well-a-day for the grand old days ?
The world is the same, if the bard has an aim,
   By the flowing River of Aise.

" There's beauty and love, and truth and power.
   Cease well-a-day for the old, old days !
The humblest home is worth Greece and Rome,
   By the flowing River of Aise.

" There are themes enough for the poet's strains.
   Leave well-a-day for the quaint old days !
Take thine eyes from the ground ; look up and around,
   By the flowing River of Aise.

"To-day is as grand as the centuries past ;
   Leave well-a-day for the famed old days !
There are wrongs to right, there are battles to fight,
   By the flowing River of Aise.

" There are hearts as true to love, to strive :
  No well-a-day for the dark old days !
Go put into type the age that is ripe,
  By the flowing River of Aise."

Then the merry poet sang down the vale,
  " Farewell, farewell to the dead old days ! "
By day and by night, there is music and light
  By the flowing River of Aise.

WHY?

I.

THE old and melancholy truth
Still haunts the hours of age and youth.
The world's great problem on our dreams
Falls freezing like the ice on streams.
The vision sweet, the bitter fact ;
The promise large, the meagre act ;
The glorious hope, the sigh of pain, —
Like wave on wave, with old refrain
Sound on, again and yet again.

O wise philosopher ! too well
Upon our ears your reasoning fell ;
Too easily the doors you ope
That lead into our boundless hope.
The road to light is not so cheap ;
The hills are rough, the vales are steep.

You see not that within each breast
Is rooted deep the great Unrest, —
The god within a prison pent,
That may not yield to argument.
Your proofs we cannot well deny,
Yet clings behind the unsolaced Why.
We strain our vision to the end ;
We trust we love the heavenly Friend ;
We sun our thoughts in Being's beam, —
And wake to find our faith a dream.

Why was I born, and where was I
Before this living mystery
That weds the body to the soul ?
What are the laws by whose control
I live and feel and think and know ?
What the allegiance that I owe
To tides beyond all time and space ?
What form of faith must I embrace ?
Why thwarted, starved, and overborne
By fate, — an exile, driven forlorn
By fitful winds, where each event
Seems but the whirl of accident ?
Why feel our wings so incomplete,
Or, flying, but a plumed deceit,

Renewing all our lives to us
The fable old of Icarus?

Tell me the meaning of the breath
That whispers from the house of death,
That chills thought's metaphysic strife,
That dims the dream of After-life.
Why, if we lived not ere our birth,
Hope for a state beyond this earth?
Tell me the secret of the hope
That gathers, as we upwards ope
The skylights of the prisoned soul
Unto the perfect and the whole.
Yet why the loveliest things of earth
Mock in their death their glorious birth.
Why, when the scarlet sunset floods
The west beyond the hills and woods,
Or June with roses crowds my porch,
Or northern lights with crimson torch
Illume the snow and veil the stars
With streaming bands and wavering bars,
Or music's sensuous, soul-like wine
Intoxicates with trance divine, —
Why then must sadness like a thief
Steal my aromas of belief,

And like a cloud that shuts the day
At sunrise, turn my gold to gray ?

Tell me why instincts meant for good
Turn to a madness of the blood ;
And, baffling all our morals nice,
Nature seems nearly one with vice.
What sin and misery mean, if blent
With good in one divine intent.
Why from such source must evil spring,
And finite still mean suffering ?

Thus ever questioning we stand,
As though upon some alien land,
And grope for truth beyond our reach,
Through foreign modes and unknown speech.
One mystery above, below,
Within, o'erveiling all we know.
What riddle harder to unwind
Than man himself can man e'er find ?
Wiser than prophet and than sage
Must be the eye that reads this page, —
The enigma of the double soul, —
This angel-devil, half and whole,
Whose eye is filled with wisdom's light,

Whose lips are breathing lust and spite;
The dim vaults of whose heart and brain
Heaven's warmth, hell's heat at once contain.
The isolated text is he
For clashing creeds and prophecy;
The sibyl-leaf that winds have whirled
About the corners of the world;
A scrap, a hint, that chance has swept
Out of the book the heavens have kept.
How can we know, — forlorn we cry, —
Our origin, our destiny ?
What need to strive, — we ask, — so fast
The web of fate is o'er us cast ?
Why, if the authentic seal we wear,
Should we prove aught than good and fair ?

Look on the millions born to blight;
The souls that pine for warmth and light;
The crushed and stifled swarms that pack
The foul streets and the alleys black, —
The miserable lives that crawl
Outside the grim partition wall
'Twixt rich and poor, 'twixt foul and fair,
'Twixt vaulting hope and lame despair.
On that wall's sunny side, within,

Hang ripening fruits and tendrils green,
O'er garden-beds of bloom and spice,
And perfume as of paradise.
There happy children run and talk
Along the shade-flecked gravel-walk,
And lovers sit in rosy bowers,
And music overflows the hours,
And wealth and health and mirth and books
Make pictures in Arcadian nooks.
But on that wall's grim outer stones
The fierce north-wind of winter groans ;
Through blinding dust, o'er bleak highway,
The slant sun's melancholy ray
Sees stagnant pool and poisonous weed,
The hearts that faint, the feet that bleed,
The grovelling aim, the flagging faith,
The starving curse, the drowning death !

O wise philosopher ! you soothe
Our troubles with a touch too smooth.
Too plausibly your reasonings come.
They will not guide me to my home ;
They lead me on a little way
Through meadows, groves, and gardens gay,
Until a wall shuts out my day, —

A screen whose top is hid in clouds,
Whose base is deep on dead men's shrouds.
Could I dive under pain and death,
Or mount and breathe the whole heaven's breath,
I might begin to comprehend
How the Beginning joins the End.

Like one who wanders where he lists
In some enchanted land of mists,
Mid mighty temples to explore
Of hieroglyphs the hidden lore,
Or forms of demigods to trace
Carved on the crumbling ruin's face : —
He sees the sculptured column stand,
With bas-reliefs wrought, small or grand ;
In spiral bands the heroic troops
Circling the shaft in crowded groups ;
But, gazing up, sees not at all
The mist-enshrouded capital,
And cornice, frieze, and architrave
Sleep buried in one cloudy grave.
We agonize in doubt, perplexed
O'er fate, free-will, and Bible-text.
In vain.   The spirit finds no vent
From out the imprisoning temperament.

Philosophies that stalk in pride
Seem but our shadows magnified ;
Windows of many-colored glass
Tinting all thoughts that through us pass ;
And Revelation but a name
For the intense grand tones that came
To a few saints whose ears were fine,
In old and distant Palestine.
Truth, truth, God's truth ! naught else, — we cry ;
For somewhere in the earth and sky
The master-mind must lurk, whose word
Sounds the keynote of all accord.
Give us thyself, O godlike Truth !
Thy blood-warm veins, thy kiss of youth.
Flit not in many-colored light ;
Shine clear, as to the All-seeing Sight.

II.

Yet why should we forever press and dent
The brain with ceaseless blows of argument ?
Why overstrain the object-wearied sight,
Nor rest content with passages of light ?
Perhaps it seems that we are backward thrust
From God, that, toiling upward through the dust,
Groping our blindfold way to Truth and Him,

Excess of glory may not pain or dim
The eyes that must be daily trained to see
The full-orbed truths that type the Deity,
Who overcasts his splendors to ensnare
His children in the good and true and fair.

Say blest Illusion, that hoodwinks our eyes,
And veils for us the overpowering skies,
And lights a fire that only cheers and warms.
God weds our souls to undeveloped forms,
And tempers his great lights, which, too intense
For untried eyes, might blind, or craze the sense.
O burning day-star! could the Parsee old
Have worshipped thee, save that with fold on fold
Of space and air the intolerable fire
Were fitted to the limits of desire?
O sacred boundaries 'twixt unknown and known!
O wholesome stringency of nature's zone!
Spirit immersed in form, that form may know
Its source, through growth and spiritual throe,
And work together with the all-circling law
That knows no lapse, no accident, no flaw!
So, step by step, through tortuous ways we grope,
Becalmed by faith, blown on by fitful hope;
The vast light-region ne'er entirely hid,

Still shimmering through the labyrinths we thrid ;
Still glittering on the angles that project
Along our cavern windings, and protect
Our stumbling steps, nor suffer that we run
Like candle-blinded moths into the sun.
The Himalayan heights are kindly screened ;
Their upward sloping bases over-greened
With flowery paths and arbors here and there
For noontide rest ; and vistas opening fair,
Where birds are carolling through boughs and vines,
And odors of the aromatic pines.

Therefore I bow my spirit to the Power
That underflows and fills my little hour.
I feel the eternal symphony afloat,
In which I am a breath, a passing note.
I may be but a dull and jarring nerve
In the great body, yet some end I serve.

Yea, though I dream and question still the dream
Thus floating by me upon Being's stream,
Some end I serve.   Love reigns.   I cannot lose
The Primal Light, though thousand-fold its hues.
I can believe that somewhere Truth abides ;
Not in the ebb and flow of those small tides

That float the dogmas of our saints and sects ;
Not in a thousand tainted dialects,
But in the one pure language, could we hear,
That fills with love and light the seraphs' sphere.
I can believe there is a Central Good,
That burns and shines o'er temperament and mood ;
That somewhere God will melt the clouds away,
And his great purpose shine as shines the day.
Then may we know why now we could not know ;
Why the great Isis-curtain drooped so low ;
Why we were blindfold on a path of light ;
Why came wild gleams and voices through the night ;
Why we seemed drifting, storm-tost, without rest,
And were but rocking on a Mother's breast.

THROUGH THE FIELDS TO ST. PETER'S.

THERE's a by-road to St. Peter's.   First you swing
   across the Tiber
 In a ferry-boat that floats you in a minute from the
   crowd :
Then through high-hedged lanes you saunter; then by
   fields and sunny pastures ;
 And beyond the wondrous dome uprises like a golden
   cloud.

And this morning, Easter morning, while the streets
   were thronged with people,
 And all Rome moved toward the apostle's temple by
   the usual way,
I strolled by the fields and hedges, stopping now to view
   the landscape,
 Now to sketch the lazy cattle in the April grass that lay.

Galaxies of buttercups and daisies ran along the
    meadows,
  Rosy flushes of red clover, blossoming shrubs and
    sprouting vines.
Overhead the larks were singing, heeding not the bells
    a-ringing,
  Little knew they of the *Pasqua*, or the proud St. Peter's
    shrines.

Contadini, men and women, in their very best apparel
  Trooping one behind another, chatted all along the
    roads.
Boys were pitching quoits and coppers, old men in the
    sun were basking.
  In the festal smile of Heaven all laid aside their weary
    loads.

Underneath an ancient portal soon I passed into the
    city ;
  Entered San Pietro's Square, now thronged with
    upward crowding forms,
Past the Cardinals' gilded coaches, and the gorgeous
    scarlet lackeys,
  And the flashing files of soldiers, and black priests in
    gloomy swarms.

All were moving to the temple.   Push aside the ponder-
    ous curtain ;
    Lo ! the glorious heights of marble, melting in the
       golden dome,
Where the grand mosaic pictures, veiled in warm and
    misty softness,
    Swim in faith's religious trances, high above all heights
      of Rome.

Grand as Pergolesi chantings, lovely as a dream of Titian,
    Tones and tints and chastened splendors wreathed and
      grouped in sweet accord ;
While through nave and transept pealing, soar and sink
    the choral voices,
    Telling of the death and glorious resurrection of the
      Lord.

But, ah, fatal degradation for this temple of the na-
    tions !
    For the soul is never lifted by the accord of sights and
      sound,
But yon priest in gold and satin, mumming with his
    ghostly Latin,
    Drags it from its natural flights, and trails its plumage
      on the ground.

And to-day the Pope is heading his whole army of gay
 puppets,
  And the great machinery moving round us with an
  extra show :
Genuflections, censers, mitres, mystic motions, candle-
 lighters,
  And the juggling show of relics to the crowd that
  gapes below ;

Till at last they show the Pontiff, draped and diademed
 and tinselled,
  Under canopy and fan-plumes borne along in splendor
  proud
To a show-box of the temple overlooking all the Piazza.
  There he gives his benediction to the long-expectant
  crowd.

Benediction ! while this people, blighted, cursed by
 superstition,
  Steeped in ignorance and darkness, taxed and starved,
  looks up and begs
For a little light and freedom, for a little law and
 justice,
  That at least the cup so bitter they may drain not to
  the dregs.

Benediction! while old Error keeps alive a nameless
terror.
Benediction! while the poison at each pore is entering
deep,
And the sap is slowly withered, and the wormy fruit is
gathered,
And a vampire sucks the life out, while the soul is
fanned asleep!

Ah! this splendor gluts the senses, while the spirit pines
and dwindles.
Mother Church is but a dry-nurse, singing while her
infant moans;
While anon a cake or rattle gives a little half-oblivion,
And the sweetness and the glitter mingle with her
drowsy tones.

But the infant moans and tosses with a nameless want
and anguish,
While with coarse unmeaning hushings louder sings
the hireling nurse;
Knows no better in her dull and superannuated blind-
ness,
Tries no potion, seeks no nurture, but consents to
worse and worse.

If such be thy ultimation, Church of infinite preten-
    sion, —
  If within thy chosen garden flowers and fruits like
    these be found,
Ah, give me the book of nature, open wide to every
    creature,
  And the unconsecrated thoughts that spring like
    daisies all around.

Send me to the woods and waters, to the studio, to the
    market ;
  Give me simple conversation, books, arts, sports, and
    friends sincere.
Let no priest be e'er my tutor, on my brow no label
    written ;
  Coin or passport to salvation rather none than ask
    it here.

Give me air, and not a prison ; love for heart, and light
    for reason.
  Let me walk no slave or bigot,— God's untrammelled,
    fearless child.
Yield me rights each soul is born to, — rights not given
    and not taken,
  Free to cardinals and princes, and Campagna shepherds
    wild.

Like these Roman fountains gushing clear and sweet in
    open spaces,
  Where the poorest beggar stoops to drink, and none
    can say him nay,
Let the law, the truth, be common, free to man and child
    and woman, —
  Living waters for the souls that now in sickness waste
    away.

Therefore are these fields far sweeter than yon temple of
    St. Peter.
  Through this grander dome of azure God looks down
    and blesses all.
In these fields the birds sing clearer, to the Eternal Heart
    are nearer,
  Than the proud monastic chants that yonder on my
    ears did fall.

Never smiled Christ's holy vicar on the heretic and sinner
  As this sun, true type of Godhead, smiles o'er all the
    peopled land.
Sweeter smells this blowing clover than the perfume of
    the censer,
  And the touch of spring is kinder than the pontiff's
    jewelled hand.

    ROME, Easter, 1859.

MARION DALE.

—————

MARION DALE, I remember you once
    In the days when you blushed like a rose half blown,
Long ere that wealthy respectable dunce
    Sponged up your beautiful name in his own.

I remember you, Marion Dale,
    So artless and cordial, so modest and sweet;
You did not walk in that glittering mail
    That covers you now from your head to your feet.

Well I remember your welcoming smile
    When Alice and Annie and Edward and I
Walked over to see you, — you lived but a mile
    From my uncle's old house and the grove that stood
        nigh.

I was no lover of yours (pray excuse me);
    You and I differed on many a view.

I never gave you a chance to refuse me,
　　Already I loved one less changeful than you.

Still it was ever a pride and a pleasure
　　Just to be near you, the rose of our vale.
Often I thought, " Who will own such a treasure ?
　　Who win the fresh heart of our Marion Dale ? "

I wonder now if you ever remember,
　　Ever sigh over fifteen years ago ;
Whether your June is all turned to December ;
　　Whether your hopes are rewarded, or no.

Gone are those winters of chats and of dances,
　　Gone are those summers of picnics and rides ;
Gone the aroma of life's young romances,
　　Gone the swift flow of our passionate tides.

Marion Dale, no longer our Marion,
　　You have gone your way, and I have gone mine.
Lowly I 've labored, while fashion's gay clarion
　　Sounded your name through the waltz and the wine.

Now, when I meet you, your smile it is colder ;
　　Statelier, prouder, your features have grown ;
Rounder each white and magnificent shoulder ;
　　Barer your bosom than once, I must own.

Jewelled and satined, your tresses gold-netted,
  Queenly mid flattering voices you move;
Half to your own native graces indebted,
  Half to the station and fortune you love.

" Marion " we called you.   My wife was " dear Alice."
  I was plain Phil.   We were intimate all.
Strange, as we send in our cards at your palace,
  For " Mrs. Prime Goldbanks of Bubblemere Hall."

Six golden lackeys illumine the doorway.
  Sure, one would think, by the glances they throw,
We had slid down from the mountains of Norway,
  And had forgotten to shake off the snow.

They will permit us to enter, however;
  Usher us into her splendid saloon.
There we sit waiting and waiting forever,
  As one would watch for the rise of the moon.

'T is n't, we know, her great day for receiving;
  Still she 's at home, and a little unbends.
While she is dressing, perhaps she is weaving
  Some speech that will suit her " American friends."

Smiling you meet us, but not quite sincerely.
    Low-voiced you greet us, but this is the *ton*.
This, we must feel it, is courtesy merely,
    Not the glad welcome of days that are gone.

We are in England, — the land where they freeze one,
    When they 've a mind to, with fashion and form.
Yet, if you choose, you can thoroughly please one.
    Currents run through you, still youthful and warm.

So one would think at least, seeing you moving
    Radiant and gay at the Countess's *fête*.
Was all that babble so very improving ?
    Where was the charm, that you lingered so late ?

Ah ! well enough, as you dance on in joyance ;
    Still well enough, at your dinners and calls.
Fashion and riches will mask much annoyance.
    Float on, fair lady, whatever befalls.

Yet, Lady Marion, for hours and for hours
    You are alone with your husband and lord.
There is a skeleton hid in yon flowers,
    There is a spectre at bed and at board.

Needs no confessing to tell there is acting
　　Somewhere about you a tragedy grim.
All your bright rays have a sullen refracting;
　　Everywhere looms up the image of him, —

Him whom you love not; — there is no concealing.
　　How could you love him apart from his gold?
Nothing now left but your firefly wheeling,
　　Flashing one moment, then pallid and cold.

Yet you 've accepted the life that he offers;
　　Sunk to his level, not raised him to yours.
All your fair flowers have their roots in his coffers.
　　Empty the gold-dust — and then what endures?

So then we leave you.　Your world is not ours.
　　Alice and I will not trouble you more.
Not like your spring is the scent of these flowers
　　Down the broad stairway.　Quick, open the door!

Here in the free air we 'll pray for you, lady, —
　　You who are changed to us, gone from us, lost.
Soon the Atlantic will part us, already
　　Parted by gulfs that can never be crossed.

VEILS.

ONCE we called each other friends.
   'T. was no formal greeting
When we clasped each other's hands;
   Soul with soul came meeting.
Long ago I loved your books,
   (They first drew me to you);
Loved you better than you thought;
   Ere I saw you knew you.
Other friends now come between,
   Other love outstrips me.
Can my light be then so dull
   That they all eclipse me?
Often have I longed for you;
   Often have I wondered
Why we two, whose thoughts were one,
   Ever should be sundered.

There are those who cling to you
　　As their lamp and fuel,
Or who wear you on their fronts
　　Like a glittering jewel;
Those who think to gild their rust
　　With your fame's reflection,
Vainly dreaming that they stand
　　In your best affection ;
Happy if they can be seen
　　With you closely talking,
Proud, if arm in arm with you
　　In the street, they 're walking.
Though they press so near, and live
　　In your smiles and glances,
Never are they so near as one
　　Linked with all your fancies, —
One who reads the Poet's thought
　　Through his pages gleaming,
Following him from depth to depth
　　In his subtlest dreaming ;
And who feels in firm accord
　　Listener and singer, —
Vibrating beneath your touch —
　　Bell-chimes to the ringer.

Yet I never said how much
    All your poems moved me.
Love, I said, must answer love,
    For I thought you loved me.

Time and space and circumstance
    Barred me from your presence.
Then behind your veils you seemed
    Some dim phosphorescence.
Half-transparent window-shades
    Told where you were sitting,
And your astral lamp, half blurred,
    Threw your shadow flitting
Up against the curtain-folds.
    " There," I said, " his place is."
Soon came other silhouettes,
    But all stranger-faces.
Said I : " He is feasting there
    Friends for this night only.
When the guests are gone, he 'll come
    Where I 'm waiting lonely ; —
Waiting, leaning at the door,
    While his intonations
Rise and fall for other ears.
    So I wait with patience.

For that voice I know so well,
　　With those merry fellows,
Talks for them, but sings for me :
　　Can I then be jealous ?
When the festal lights are out,
　　And heaven's stars are shining,
He will clasp me by the hand.
　　Arm in arm entwining,
We will pace his garden-walks,
　　Of the past discoursing.
All his heart will open, free
　　From convention's forcing.
As old friends who feel no cloud
　　Overcast their greeting,
Such shall be our cordial grasp,
　　Such our joyous meeting.
Ah, the pleasant dream is o'er !
　　Now his guests are going,
He but stands upon the step ;
　　And a wind is blowing
Somewhat chill between his words,
　　Which to me are sorrow.
For he saith, " 'T is very late ;
　　Can you come to-morrow ? '

Ah, to-morrow, dreary word !
  When we feel " Now only."
And the bolt slides in the door,
  And the night is lonely.
And not e'en these parting guests
  Deign a conversation.
Theirs the warm adieu of love,
  Mine its desolation.

" Were we far from fashion's forms,
  In some desert gloomy,
You might learn to know me then ;
  For you never knew me !
Time and space will now build up
  The old wall between us.
Can the sculptor warm to life
  His cold marble Venus ?
Fate has given one world to you,
  And to me another.
We can never cross her bars,
  Though you were my brother.
On your hearth the fires will glow,
  I shall see the ashes ;
All that I shall know of you
  Will be distant flashes.

I will read your books again ;
　　They at least will lead me
Into walks where we may meet,
　　Though you do not need me.
I will fancy you the same
　　As in that bright weather
Ere this cold estrangement came, —
　　You and 1 together.
You and I will speak in dreams
　　Loves not unrequited,
As we met ten years ago,
　　Happy and united."

Rome, 1859.

THE SPIRIT OF THE AGE.

A WONDROUS light is filling the air,
And rimming the clouds of the old despair;
And hopeful eyes look up to see
Truth's mighty electricity, —
Auroral shimmerings swift and bright,
That wave and flash in the silent night, —
Magnetic billows travelling fast,
And flooding all the spaces vast
From dim horizon to farthest cope
Of heaven, in streams of gathering hope.
Silent they mount and spread apace,
And the watchers see old Europe's face
Lit with expression new and strange, —
The prophecy of coming change.

Meantime, while thousands, wrapt in dreams,
Sleep heedless of the electric gleams,

Or ply their wonted work and strife,
Or plot their pitiful games of life ;
While the emperor bows in his formal halls,
And the clerk whirls on at the masking balls ;
While the lawyer sits at his dreary files,
And the banker fingers his glittering piles,
And the priest kneels down at his lighted shrine,
And the fop flits by with his mistress fine, —
The diplomat works at his telegraph wires :
His back is turned to the heavenly fires.
Over him flows the magnetic tide,
And the candles are dimmed by the glow outside.
Mysterious forces overawe,
Absorb, suspend the usual law.
The needle stood northward an hour ago ;
Now it veers like a weathercock to and fro.
The message he sends flies not as once ;
The unwilling wires yield no response.
Those iron veins that pulsed but late
From a tyrant's will to a people's fate,
Flowing and ebbing with feverish strength,
Are seized by a Power whose breadth and length,
Whose height and depth, defy all gauge
Save the great spirit of the age.
The mute machine is moved by a law

5 *

That knows no accident or flaw,
And the iron thrills to a different chime
Than that which rang in the dead old time.
For Heaven is taking the matter in hand,
And baffling the tricks of the tyrant band.
The sky above and the earth beneath
Heave with a supermundane breath.
Half-truths, for centuries kept and prized,
By higher truths are polarized.
Like gamesters on a railroad train,
Careless of stoppage, sun or rain,
We juggle, plot, combine, arrange,
And are swept along by the rapid change.
And some who from their windows mark
The unwonted lights that flood the dark,
Little by little, in slow surprise
Lift into space their sleepy eyes;
Little by little are made aware
That a spirit of power is passing there, —
That a spirit is passing, strong and free, —
The soul of the nineteenth century.

PARIS, February, 1860.

ATALANTA.

WE read in classic legends old
Of one who, fair and overbold,
Distanced all runners, till outrun by gold.

Supple in limb, and fair in face,
She passed the swiftest in the race,
Till on one luckless day she lost her place.

There came to her a cunning fellow,
His pockets stuffed with apples mellow,—
Pure gold they were, of Californian yellow.

Doffing his hat, " Fair dame," said he,
" They say thou art the fastest she
That ever ran a rig.   Wilt run with me ?

" I know the law prescribed," he said :
" If you should beat, I lose my head ;
But if you are beaten, you and I must wed."

Away his hat he swiftly twirls.
The fleetest of all swift-limbed girls
Tosses her head with all its sunny curls.

Then, One — two — three! Away they fly.
Together for a while they ply
Their agile feet. Then soon she passes by.

But will she win? A ball of gold
Hippomenes has deftly rolled
Along the course. She stoops. Her apron's fold

Contains the prize. Another ball
Of dazzling value he lets fall,
And yet a third. She stops to gather all.

So Atalanta lost her race
And single blessedness, to chase
Three rolling lumps of metal, bright but base.

Now list, Columbia, to my moral.
Thou runnest well. Don't stop to quarrel
About thy baser wealth. Prefer a laurel.

The fleetest in the race are lost,
If in their gold alone they boast.
Be wiser thou, and count the entire cost.

The nations feel thee great.   All eyes
Watch thy swift motions with surprise,
And hail thee herald of unclouded skies.

Be great in soul, as great in power ;
Be rich in minds, Heaven's richest dower ;
So of all nations thou shalt be the flower.

AL HASSAN'S SECRET.

You may tell me that the priests of Egypt,
Muttering charms and raising magic terrors,
Breathed it through him in their tombs and caverns,
Stamped it on him with the seal of silence
And the dread of excommunication.
You may say he heard it on the river,
In the Nile froth by the low shore lapping
In and out among the reeds and rushes;
In the moaning of the lurid sand-storm;
In a noon-dream mid the rustling palm-tufts,
Whispered by the sun-scorched leaves above him.
I, who know so well the Sheik Al Hassan,
I, the poet Yefid, can assure you
Sheik Al Hassan is no vision-seër;
Fears no priests, but laughs at all their juggles;
In the desert never met a Geni;
Worships in the mosque no power but Allah.

Yet Al Hassan has one awful secret,
Known to him alone of all his people, —
Some strange word forbidden to be uttered;
For, if spoken, all the established order
Built upon the solid past would tremble,
Pass, perchance, in chaos and confusion,
And another law control the nations.
What this potent word may be I know not.
How it came to him he never told me.
I his bosom friend have never heard it;
In my deepest thoughts I cannot guess it,
Though long silent days we ride together.

But one night I ever shall remember.
After toiling through the powdery desert,
We were resting in the grove of Kamah.
Clear as noonday shone the wondrous moonlight.
In our tent we slept, but woke together.
Overhead one feathery palm-tree rustled;
On the white tent lay its shortened shadow,
And the shadow's waving fringes trembled
On the tent-roof, darkening all one corner.
Grouped around the weary camels slumbered,
And the turbaned slaves. A fountain gurgled,
Hid in darkness, while its tiny streamlet

H

Trickled silvery sparkles o'er the pebbles.
On the grass lay shadow-blots fantastic,
Mixed with moon-gold rounded into circles.

In that moonlight there we woke together,
Suddenly, as if a voice had called us ;
Broad awake, as if a spirit passed us.
Something whispered that the air was haunted
With a presence vaguely brooding o'er us,
Pressing close, until the nerves all tingled
Tense and trembling, as a wind-harp shivers
In the coming breeze of autumn evenings,
Ere the first wild minor chords are wakened.
So I lay and stared upon the whiteness
Of the ghostly tent, and on the shadows
On the tent-floor creeping like black fingers ;
Till at length Al Hassan broke the silence.

" Could I tell to thee, O son of music,
Could I tell the secret of my bosom,
Ah, what pain, what pain would here be softened !
What a light o'er weary days would brighten !
Could I only shape it in some fashion,
Temper the fierce light to misty softness,

Dwarf the giant's supermundane stature,
As the fisherman enclosed the Geni
In the box he carried on his shoulders,
It would flush the desert of my bosom
With a sudden burst of flowers and fountains."

Was I waking then, or was I dreaming,
Or enchanted ?   " Know," he said, " O Yefid,
Good and evil in this word are mingled.
Like the angel of the summer lightning,
Cloud-winged, scowling o'er the mountain cedars,
Darting bolts of death, yet breathing freshness ;
So the truth — if truth it be I harbor
In my burdened breast — a double message
On its wings would bear unto my people.
Some must take the good and some the evil
Dropped from either wing of this strange angel.

" Yet could I, the prophet's weakest servant,
Seize that faith which, means to ends subjecting,
Seeing in the madly shattered systems
But the opening of the eternal order ; —
Faith of prophets and of wonder-workers,
In whose white light dazzling and o'erwhelming,

Death is but a spot we hardly notice,
And destruction but the broom that sweeping
Clears the spaces for God's mighty building, —
Then I might perhaps forsake my desert ;
Bear my smothered torch among the cities ;
Stand and see the mighty visitation,
The veiled messenger of good and evil
Shaking dew and fire from either pinion ;
Watch the firebrand kindling in their houses
Till they walked by light of conflagrations ;
Hear the trumpets of divine destroyers
Blaring through the market and the palace ; —
Had I only faith ; — and yet I tremble,
Scarce even daring to myself to whisper
What would soon rebound in shocks of thunder ;
So unlike the language of the present,
So profane perhaps, so wild, that madmen
Might essay to mumble it, half dreaming,
While the sane ones passed them with a shudder.
I, alas, am all too weak and faithless
For a mission of so huge a burden.
I am not a sage to explain its meaning,
Nor a saint to avouch its truth unflinching,
Ready for the fate of God's great martyrs.
Though a voice cries, " Speak," I falter, tremble,

Turn away, and carry through the desert
Strange, dumb pain that crowds my heart to bursting."

So Al Hassan from his couch half risen
Poured his sad speech, while the palm-tree's shadow
Crept upon him, and the tent grew darker.

Then I said : " Tell me alone the secret,
Only me, the strange wild word, not fearing ;
So thou drawest the arrow from thy bosom,
While I heal the wound with love's own balsam.
In the desert here no traitor listens ;
Let us share the mystery and the sorrow."
" Never, O my Yefid ! " was his answer.
" No ; too well I love thee, dearest poet,
With a heedless hand to blight our friendship.
Better bear alone the fated burden,
Than for one brief moment's consolation
Turn my friend into my bitter foeman."

Then upon his couch Al Hassan turned him,
Sighed a deep, long sigh, and watched the moonlight
Pave the tent-floor with its golden patches.

I am wondering still, and dare not question
What the fatal word is.   Word of Heaven —
May it not be so ? — if such the ending
In the birth-throes of a new creation.
I am wondering still, but cannot guess it;
While Al Hassan rides upon his camel
Over the desert, like a statue haunted.

MY OLD PALETTE.

MANY a year has fled away
   Since this old palette was new,
As may be seen by the spots of green
   And yellow and red and blue.

Many a picture was painted from this,
   While many were only dreamed ;
And shadow and light like the black and white
   Across my life have streamed.

Accept, my friend, this plain old board
   All plastered and imbrowned,
Where the pleasure and strife of a painter's life
   Have left a mosaic ground.

The color that went to the picture's soul
   Has left but its body behind ;
Yet strive to trace on its cloudy face
Some gleam of the artist's mind.

And think of the friend upon whose thumb
   This brown old tablet hung,
And the baffled aim, where visions came
   Unpainted and unsung.

Mine be the records all obscure
   Upon the surface blent;
Be yours the love that seeks to prove
   My deed by my intent.

1866.

THE BOBOLINKS.

WHEN Nature had made all her birds,
   With no more cares to think on,
She gave a rippling laugh, and out
   There flew a Bobolinkon.

She laughed again ; out flew a mate :
   A breeze of Eden bore them
Across the fields of Paradise,
   The sunrise reddening o'er them.

Incarnate sport and holiday,
   They flew and sang forever ;
Their souls through June were all in tune,
   Their wings were weary never.

Their tribe, still drunk with air and light,
   And perfume of the meadow,
Go reeling up and down the sky,
   In sunshine and in shadow.

One springs from out the dew-wet grass;
　　Another follows after;
The morn is thrilling with their songs
　　And peals of fairy laughter.

From out the marshes and the brook,
　　They set the tall reeds swinging,
And meet, and frolic in the air,
　　Half prattling and half singing.

When morning winds sweep meadow-lands
　　In green and russet billows,
And toss the lonely elm-tree's boughs,
　　And silver all the willows,

I see you buffeting the breeze,
　　Or with its motion swaying,
Your notes half drowned against the wind,
　　Or down the current playing.

When far away o'er grassy flats,
　　Where the thick wood commences,
The white-sleeved mowers look like specks
　　Beyond the zigzag fences,

And noon is hot, and barn-roofs gleam
    White in the pale blue distance,
I hear the saucy minstrels still
    In chattering persistence.

When Eve her domes of opal fire
    Piles round the blue horizon,
Or thunder rolls from hill to hill
    A Kÿrie Eleison,

Still merriest of the merry birds,
    Your sparkle is unfading; —
Pied harlequins of June, — no end
    Of song and masquerading.

What cadences of bubbling mirth,
    Too quick for bar and rhythm!
What ecstasies, too full to keep
    Coherent measure with them !

O could I share, without champagne
    Or muscadel, your frolic,
The glad delirium of your joy,
    Your fun un-apostolic,

Your drunken jargon through the fields,
   Your bobolinkish gabble,
Your fine Anacreontic glee,
   Your tipsy reveller's babble!

Nay, let me not profane such joy
   With similes of folly ;
No wine of earth could waken songs
   So delicately jolly!

O boundless self-contentment, voiced
   In flying air-born bubbles !
O joy that mocks our sad unrest,
   And drowns our earth-born troubles !

Hope springs with you : I dread no more
   Despondency and dulness ;
For Good Supreme can never fail,
   That gives such perfect fulness.

The life that floods the happy fields
   With song and light and color
Will shape our lives to richer states,
   And heap our measures fuller.

1866.

CRETE.

———

SPERANZA, Speranza! we felt through the night-time
   The thrill of thy voice and the joy of thy lyre;
Heard thee far off singing sweet of the bright time
   Prophets foretold in their large heart's desire.

Strains floated by in the sad waning moonlight,
   While we stood calling thy name from afar.
Come to thy summer bowers, queen of high noonlight,
   Full-armed and splendid, — our souls' morning-star!

Come as thou camest when Italy panted
   And leapt to her feet, o'er her dukes and her kings.
Come, like the new life America planted
   To blossom and yield through her ages of springs.

Come to the spirits benighted, unlettered,
   Unbarring the portals of science and love.
Come to the bodies enslaved, tasked and fettered;
   Build up the freedom no tyrant can move.

O, they are grappling for life, — just for breathing ;
    Hoping naught, asking naught, — only to stand ;
Only to stand with their arms interwreathing,
    Brotherlike, bound to their own fatherland.

Faintly they hear thee.   "Speranza, Speranza !"
    They call in the gloom.   Are the echoes all dead ?
Comes there no voice from Mount Ida in answer ?
    Shines there no star in the pale morning-red ?

Must the fierce ranks of the Ottoman Nero
    Trample their life out with barbarous feet ?
Is there no god, no Olympian hero,
    Left on thy mountains, O desolate Crete ?

O shame on the nations who sent the Crusaders
    To wrest from the Turk the dead stones of a tomb,
Yet give a live race to the savage invaders,
    And lift not a finger to lighten its gloom !

And shame to proud France, who has opened with greeting
    To the red-handed tyrant her welcoming doors ;
And shame to old England, that welcome repeating,
    That brings the crowned butcher a guest to her shores !

Ah, well ! Heaven wills that the selfish should blunder.
   The tyrants are deaf, but the people know well
How God in the heavens sits holding the thunder
   That strikes to its centre the kingdom of hell.

For sooner or later — no seer can foreknow it —
   Falls the swift bolt, and the thrones are ablaze.
Time yet shall re-echo the lay of the poet,
   And Greece shall live over her happiest days.

J. R. L.

On his Fiftieth Birthday, Feb. 22, 1869.

At fifty years, how many frosty polls
　We see, whose wintry solitude begins;
How many faces hard as Chaldee scrolls,
　Crowfeet on parchment skins.

At fifty, Time has picked our thickest locks;
　Polished the outer, dulled the inner head;
Filched golden dreams from many a knowledge-box,
　And left dry facts instead.

Old beaux, not Cupid's, are at fifty bent,
　With stooping shoulders and with shambling gait;
Their sinew strings all slack, their arrows spent,
　Their quivers desolate.

At fifty, scholars cease to dream, whose youth
　Teemed with live thoughts, and generous hopes of man;
All influx fresh of beauty and of truth
　Shut out as by a ban:

Cramped by a creed that bolts its windows down
    Against the century's light and vital air, —
Their dogmas shaped by some provincial town,
    Their very gains a snare;

Life's best aroma gone, when years should claim
    The boon of calmest thought and widest scope:
The ring without the gem; a faded name;
    An epitaph on hope.

Not so the friend whose buoyant step we greet
    Rounding his hale half-century to-day,
Fresh as when earlier splendors lured his feet
    Along the enchanted way,

When o'er the land lulled to unhealthy rest
    He blew his trumpet tones or trilled his song,
Or winged his earnest arrow with a jest
    Against the shield of wrong.

The truths we scorned so long and learned so late,
    Burnt on the nation's heart by war's hot fire,
Long since he taught.   We know now how to rate
    His grave prophetic lyre.

Nor less his gayer moods, when wit and joke
   Ran flashing down his chords in humor terse
And quaint, the talk of homely Yankee folk
   Woven in sparkling verse.

His sweet enveloping fun, that wrapped the pill
   Of pungent satire, through his wise discourse
Runs fresh as ever.   Drugs that heal, not kill,
   Are his; we know their source.

He from the first wrought through his varied rhyme
   For truth, for fatherland, for freedom's cause,
As now, through riper learning, in a time
   Of better men and laws.

Grander than ever now his lyrics ring;
   His humor with a richer flavor fraught;
Sweeter the willows through his idyls sing;
   His best his latest thought.

Here under his ancestral elms we meet
   In fireside talk; and in his social lights,
Unmindful how the poet's wingéd feet
   Have trod the lonely heights,

Forget the midnight lamp, the busy brain,
  The converse with the treasures of his shelves,
And how the unconscious echo of his strain
  Makes music in ourselves.

We greet him here, still young in wit and song,
  His hair unbleached, his eye undimmed, his frame
Robust; a scholar ripe, a teacher strong,
  A bard the ages claim.

We pledge the generous heart, the exuberant soul,
  No grave professor's mask can change or hide.
One toast, "The friend we love," shall sum the whole,
  Were all that's said, denied.

For he needs not our homage or our praise:
  He lives in us; and all who know his worth.
Flatter him not with formal wreath of bays
  Grown in your Cambridge earth;

But crown him with the iris of his soul,
  Caught from the sunshine of his life and name.
Our reflex of his light the aureole
  That makes our love his fame.

SEA SHADOWS.

——

Of old the poets sang of thee, O Sea,
And peopled thee with nymphs and tritons quaint,
And fell asleep beside thy murmuring waves,
Or rocking on thy bosom, and forgot
The tiger heart that crouched and laid in wait
In seeming slumber.   Thy great glooms I sing, —
Shadows of chaos and wild passion's deeps,
And desolations of the unmeasured wastes.

O smooth, false friend, who lured us out too far
From land and home, into the realm of storms, —
Of storms and winter; or in tropic gulfs
Split our brave ships with thunderbolts; or washed
In drowning death a hundred beating hearts
With one sweep of thine arm ; or day by day
Held us in trances of long sickening calm,
Rooted in weary plains of molten glass,

Dumb with despair and famine and the dread
Of pest and fiery death, with none to help, —
The burning eye of heaven that rolled and glared
At noon, an eye of awful maniac light,
Our only witness in the unmeasured leagues
And bottomless abysses!   Thou, O Sea,
Hidest in thy blue bosom, and within
Thy gleaming bars of sand and weed-clad stones,
All haunting fears and mysteries of death,
All auguries of chaos and despair.

In thee, O melancholy mother Sea,
Lurk all the vast and direful ocean-shapes, —
The black leviathan, the ravening shark,
The huge sea-snake by mariners beheld,
The krakens and chimeras strong as death,
With elephantine tentacles and jaws
Of slow and sure destruction, and cold eyes
That fathoms down stare up and mark their prey.
Thou art the nurse of that swift cuttle-fish,
Gigantic fleshy spider of grim caves
'Neath cliffs precipitous, where sucks the tide
In snaky coils of light and dark and death,
Leagues off from land, the terror of a dream!
Thine are the shadowy waifs of shapeless growths,

Half plant, half fish, fantastic jelly forms
By moonlight drifting past old ships becalmed
In summer nights, while near the Teneriffe
The loose sails flap like thunder through the dreams
Of sleeping sailors.   Thine the gleaming teeth
Of white reefs snarling as the ships drive down
Through blackening skies.   And thine the calmer glooms
Of sad sea-beaches and their lapping waves;
The rocks half buried in the slippery heaps
Of soaking sea-weed, when the tide is low;
And, wriggling in the moonlight and the sand,
The small wet monsters crawling in and out
The hollows and the ooze; the skull-eyed rocks
With hanging tufts of yellow ocean hair
Combed by the salt winds, decked with dead old shells,
Tricked with the sad waste leavings of the storm,
And washed with treacherous kisses of the surf
That froths and sighs all night beneath the moon.

To thee I come, and scorn thy flattering kiss,
And have small faith in thy smooth surface charms.
Thou fawnest like a spaniel at my feet.
I see the wild beast in thy changeful eyes,
And trust thee not.   Rather for me the safe
Green hills and valleys of firm earth, — the joy

Of woods and pastures and the thousand homes
Lit up at evening with home-stars of love,
And musical with loving human hearts.

A truer type of power than thee I find
In the great morn of Science that hath lit
Thy shadows, and the skill that treads thee down
Into a highway for man's daily steps,
And the world's multitudinous fleets.   Three gods
Chiefly I praise, and not thy Neptune old, —
Magnet and Vapor and the Electric Fire,
Whose forces tame thy spasms, so man thy lord
May plunge across the roaring water-chasms,
And bridge the measureless, and come and go
And talk at ease across the world.

                              Thou too,
O changeful element that bore our ship
Of state upon thy breast !   We looked abroad
To thy horizon level, long, and blue
With summer skies.   We recked not of the storm,
We dreamed not of the four-years' hurricane
Raging in battle-fires, and skies of blood,
And mountain waves that swept the young and brave
To sudden death or long-drawn agonies ;
Nor saw the sunken reefs beneath the blue,

Nor the dire monsters of thy deeps, nor half
The hidden horrors of thy treacherous calms :
But trusted thee and sailed upon thy waves,
Till thy brute force turned on us, hideous, grim,
Forcing the struggle wherein wisdom rose
Triumphant.　　Thee too shall man's science tame,
Lighting the pathway o'er thy perilous deeps,
And travel forth and back across thy wastes,
And wed the sundered lands of North and South
Into one continent of flower and fruit ;
Taking away the blight of all the past,
And the blind chaos of Humanity.

THE MOUNTAIN PATH.

FAR, far above
This easy slope I gained, a mountain shines
And darkens skyward with its crags and pines;
  And upward slowly I move,

  Because I know
There is no level where I can pause, and say,
"This is sure gain."　It is too steep a way
  For mortal foot to go.

  There is no end
Of things to learn, and books to cram the brain;
They who know all, still hunger to attain.
  What boots it that they spend

  Long toiling years
To gain horizons dim and limitless?
The higher up, the more the soul's distress
  In alien atmospheres.

All is the same.
What profit hath the scholar more than I ?
Let bookworms crawl.   Better to leap or fly
With some small earnest aim.

What is the good
Of heaping pile on pile of musty lore ?
Nor paper promises, nor uncoined ore
Can buy the spirit's food.

Even the flame
Of morning burning o'er yon cedar heights
Is dull, unless an inward morn delights.
All sunshine is the same.

Our skill and wit
Snare us in useless labor and routine.
The more we search, the more retires unseen
Nature the Infinite.

The same in all.
And telescope and microscope but teach
One mystery, far above, below our reach.
There is no great or small,

No grand or mean ;
No end, and no beginning.   For we float
In Being, and learn all our creeds by rote,
    Nor see through Heaven's screen.

    This, mainly this,
We cling to, — hope that as we upward climb,
Some essence of the juices of the time,
    Some light we cannot miss,

    Gives toil its worth ;
Secretes and feeds and builds up strong and fair
The young recipient being with food and air
    Of mingled heaven and earth.

    Only what creeps
As sap from trunk to tree, from branch to flower,
Fills with the quiet plenitude of power
    The oak's unconscious deeps :

    While south-winds sift,
Rain falls and sunlight sparkles through the leaves,
And the gnarled regent of the woods receives
    The heaven's benignant gift.

What the soul needs,
It takes to itself, — aromas, sounds, and sights,
Beliefs and hopes ; finds star-tracks through the nights,
    And miracles in weeds ;

Grows unawares
To greatness, through small help and accidents,
Puzzling the pedagogue Routine, whose tents
    It leaves for manlier cares.

And by the light
Of some great law that shines on passing facts,
Some nobler purpose blending with our acts,
    We read our tasks aright ;

And gain the trust
That knowledge is best wealth.   So shall the ends
Crown the beginnings.   He who wisely spends,
    Gathers the stars as dust.

1868.

BIRD LANGUAGE.

ONE day in the bluest of summer weather,
 Sketching under a whispering oak,
I heard five bobolinks laughing together
 Over some ornithological joke.

What the fun was I could n't discover.
 Language of birds is a riddle on earth.
What could they find in whiteweed and clover
 To split their sides with such musical mirth?

Was it some prank of the prodigal summer,
 Face in the cloud or voice in the breeze,
Querulous catbird, woodpecker drummer,
 Cawing of crows high over the trees?

Was it some chipmunk's chatter, or weasel
 Under the stone-wall stealthy and sly?
Or was the joke about me at my easel,
 Trying to catch the tints of the sky?

Still they flew tipsily, shaking all over,
   Bubbling with jollity, brimful of glee,
While I sat listening deep in the clover,
   Wondering what their jargon could be.

'T was but the voice of a morning the brightest
   That ever dawned over yon shadowy hills;
'T was but the song of all joy that is lightest, —
   Sunshine breaking in laughter and trills.

Vain to conjecture the words they are singing;
   Only by tones can we follow the tune
In the full heart of the summer fields ringing,
   Ringing the rhythmical gladness of June!

THE CHANGING YEAR.

AH, fleeting year that wilt not pause a day
  To leave a picture of thy changeful moods!
Glories scarce shown and seen, and snatched away,
  Of sunsets, flushing roses, fields and woods.

The early blossoms leave the rugged thorn;
  The purple lilacs wither in the lanes;
The violets' breath, sweet for one April morn,
  Is stifled in dead leaves and drowning rains.

The chrome-gold dandelion stars of spring
  Burn out in ashy globes ere June is passed.
Too soon the hidden thrushes cease to sing,
  Too soon the summer leaves hear autumn's blast.

And ere we know, the locust's long-drawn trill
  Swells in the August noon, and nights grow cool,
And see-saw katydids foretell the chill
  Of leafless forest and of icy pool.

And flaunting golden-rods, and cardinal flowers,
    And drooping golden helmets skirt the streams,
And sighing winds give warning, and the hours
    Of sunshine waste in cloudy twilight gleams.

Yet paint thy pictures, Time, and sing thy songs !
    Thy pictures fade, thy songs die on the air.
Thou canst not take what to the soul belongs, —
    Beauty's immortal essence everywhere.

The summer goes, brown autumn treads behind,
    White winter scowls afar upon my rhyme.
I feel a Presence that is unconfined ;
    I hear a Voice whose music fills all time.

SOFT, BROWN, SMILING EYES.

SONG.

I.

SOFT, brown, smiling eyes,
　　Looking back through years,
Smiling through the mist of time,
　　Filling mine with tears,
On this sunny morn,
　　While the grape-blooms swing
In the scented air of June, —
　　Why these memories bring ?

II.

Silky rippling curls,
　　Tresses long ago
Laid beneath the shaded sod
　　Where the violets blow, —
Why across the blue
　　Of the peerless day
Do ye droop to meet my own,
　　Now all turned to gray ?

7

III.

Voice whose tender tones
  Break in sudden mirth,
Heard far back in boyhood's spring,
  Silent now on earth, —
Why so sweet and clear,
  While the bird and bee
Fill the balmy summer air,
  Come your tones to me?

IV.

Sweet, ah, sweeter far
  Than yon thrush's trill,
Sadder, sweeter than the wind,
  Woods, or murmuring rill,
Spirit words and songs
  O'er my senses creep.
Do I breathe the air of dreams?
  Do I wake or sleep?

THE DREAM OF PILATE'S WIFE.

"When Pilate was set down on the judgment-seat, his wife sent unto him, saying, 'Have thou nothing to do with that just man: for I have suffered many things this day in a dream because of him." — *Matthew* xxvii. 19. •

I KNOW my lord would laugh my dream to scorn.
He dreams no dreams; or else sees truth and dream
The same.   Why should I tell him ?   What a night !
If I should speak its visions, I believe
The very augurs would declare me mad ;
And these fanatic Jews themselves would say
No prophet of their sacred books e'er saw
In fasting trance so weird a world.

                                Methought
I stood before the Temple gates.   A vast
And wondrous moonlight flooded the huge pile,
Whose pillars gleamed with stately white and gold.
And on the steps one stood, and stretched his arms,
And called, " Come unto me, come unto me,
All ye who labor and are heavy laden,

And I will give you rest ! "   Sweet was that voice,
And plaintive, with an undertone of strength,
That thrilled the soul with strange unrest and love.
Nor less did love burn in his earnest eyes.
But all the people hurried by, and scoffed,
Or laughed.   None came to him.   None took his hand.
Yet still he stood there, like some eloquent
Grand statue of our Roman Pantheon —
But different.   Jove and Apollo thus
Never were fashioned by the sculptor's hand.

But my dream changed.   The golden moonlight paled
Under a flying scud of mist, and all
Grew black behind the Temple.   Muttering moans
Of thunder growled afar o'er Olivet.
The monumental cypresses beyond
The walls grew blacker, and the olive-trees
Tossed like gray phantoms, their huge twisted trunks
Moaning and shivering.   A great wind arose
And bore a blare of trumpets from the west,
Wailing along the sky.   Then shadowy shapes,
That seemed the semblance of an army, passed,
Tumultuous, crowding all their serried force
With chariots and with flying standards on
Into one solid thunder-cloud, whence rolled

Swift balls of fire and crashing thunder-peals,
Till the whole Temple rocked.   But in the pause
Between the peals I heard upon the steps
That voice still plaintive as a wind-harp's tone.
" Jerusalem, Jerusalem ! " it cried ;
" Thou that dost stone the prophets, thou whose hand
Nails to the bitter and the shameful cross
The bringers of good tidings, — ah, how oft
Would I have gathered thee unto my heart,
As the hen gathereth her young !   But ye
Would not.   Behold your hour has come ! "

                             And then,

The changes of my dream swept me along
Through streets I never saw, through low-arched doors,
Through cramped and tortuous caves, up marble steps,
Through royal halls that opened vistas long,
Past golden thrones, where kings and emperors
Sat mute and dead; past endless hurrying crowds,
Past gleaming files of grim centurions, —
On, till I reached a bleak and windy hill.
And some one whispered, " Golgotha ! "   There hung
The youth whom they accuse to-day, upon
The Roman gibbet.   Low his head was bowed
In agonizing death.   But slowly his form
Grew luminous, and luminous the cross,

And the great light increased till all the place
Was morning sunshine.   And, behold, the crowd
Around all vanished in the blaze.   Behold,
The pale kings crumbled on their shadowy thrones.
The iron legions blew away like smoke.
Yea, the great Temple and the city walls
And all the people faded into air.
But that strange cross, with him who hung thereon,
Grew to a blinding sun.

                Then a voice spoke, —
" The heavenly kingdom cometh upon earth.
The truth — not mine, but God's and man's — the truth
Man's soul is born to inherit as the air
And sunshine, comes not to destroy, but comes
Creating all things new, till the whole earth
Is saturated with the love of God,
And all mankind are one great family."
Then, far away, along the horizon's verge
I saw a city shining; half on earth
It seemed, and half in air.   " Perhaps," I thought,
" This is great Rome, and I shall find the house
I lived in when a girl, and shield myself
In its cool courts from this intense strange light."
And then I hurried on, o'er rugged rocks,
O'er windy plains, down valleys dim and damp,

That held the twilight all day long; till all
Grew dark about me, groping through the gloom.
Then, suddenly, a yawning precipice
Ended my flight, and giddy on its verge
I sank, and slid — down, down, clutching the air, —
Shot through with dizzy horror, — while pale forms
Of nameless terror at the bottom stood
And stretched long arms to grasp me, — when I woke.
I woke, drenched with great drops of agony;
And lay awake, counting the weird, wan hours
Of murky dawn.   I will not tell my dream
To Pilate, only that I dreamed of Him,
The wondrous teacher, suffering much in dreams.
I trust my lord will bear no part to-day
In this unhallowed trial.   Else I fear
Some hidden curse will light upon our house.
Such visions cannot be false auguries.

  1869.

THE DISPUTE OF THE SEVEN DAYS.

ONCE on a time the days of the week
    Quarrelled and made bad weather.
The point was which of the seven was best;
    So they all disputed together.

And Monday said, " I wash the clothes ";
    And Tuesday said, " I air 'em ";
And Wednesday said, " I iron the shirts ";
    And Thursday said, " I wear 'em."

And Friday, " I 'm the day for fish ";
    And Saturday, " Children love me ";
And Sunday, " I am the Sabbath day,
    I 'm sure there are none above me."

One said, " I am the fittest for work ";
    And one, " I am fittest for leisure."
Another, " I 'm best for prayer and praise ";
    And another, " I 'm best for pleasure."

Arguing thus, they flapped their wings,
   And puffed up every feather;
They blew and rained and snowed and hailed :
   There never was seen such weather.

Old Father Time was passing by,
   And heard the hurly-burly.
Said he, " Here 's something going wrong;
   It 's well I was up so early.

" These children of mine have lost their wits
   And seem to be all *non compos.*
I never knew them to gabble thus.
   Hollo there ! — stop that rumpus !

" I should think you a flock of angry geese,
   To hear your screaming and bawling.
Indeed, it would seem by the way it snows,
   Goose-feathers *are* certainly falling.

" You, Sunday, sir, with your starched cravat,
   Black coat, and church-veneering, —
Tell me the cause of this angry spat ;
   Speak loud, — I am hard of hearing.
     7 *

"You are the foremost talker here;
  The wisest sure you should be.
I little thought such a deuce of a row
  As you are all making, *could* be."

Then Sunday said, " Good Father Time,
  The case is clear as noonday;
For ever since the world was made,
  The Lord's day has been Sunday.

" The church — "   Here Monday started up:
  " The folks are glad when you leave 'em;
They all want *me* to give 'em their work,
  And the pleasures of which you bereave 'em."

But Tuesday said, " I finish your chores,
  And do them as fine as a fiddle."
And Wednesday, " I am the best of you all
  Because I stand in the middle."

And Thursday, Friday, Saturday, each
  Said things that I can't remember.
And so they might have argued their case
  From March until December.

But Father Tempus cut them short :
   " My children, why this pother ?
There is no best, there is no worst ;
   One day 's just like another.

" To God's great eye all shine alike
   As in their primal beauty.
That day is best whose deeds are best ;
   That worst that fails in duty.

" Where Justice lights the passing hours,
   Where Love is wise and tender,
There beams the radiance of the skies,
   There shines a day of splendor."

A THRUSH IN A GILDED CAGE.

WAS this the singer I had heard so long,
　　But never till this evening, face to face ?
And were they his, those tones so unlike song,
　　Those words conventional and commonplace ?

Those echoes of the usual social chat
　　That filled with noise confused the crowded hall ;
That smiling face, black coat, and white cravat ;
　　Those fashionable manners, — was this all ?

He glanced at freedmen, operas, politics,
　　And other common topics of the day ;
But not one brilliant image did he mix
　　With all the prosy things he had to say.

At least I hoped that one I long had known,
　　In the inspired books that built his fame,
Would breathe some word, some sympathetic tone,
　　Fresh from the ideal region whence he came.

And so I leave the well-dressed, buzzing crowd,
    And vent my spleen alone here by my fire;
Mourning the fading of my golden cloud,
    The disappointment of my life's desire.

Simple enthusiast! why do you require
    A budding rose for every thorny stalk?
Why must we poets always bear the lyre
    And sing, when fashion forces us to talk?

Only at moments comes the muse's light.
    Alone, like shy wood-thrushes, warble we.
Catch us in traps like this dull crowd to-night,
    We are but plain, brown-feathered birds, you see!

UNDER THE SKYLIGHT.

———

I HAVE no office with staring sign
    Down in the noise of the crowded mart.
A window square to the sky is mine
    In an humble loft, where all apart
    I live, with my friends and books and art.

No currents of gold from Wall Street come
    To breed the fever of loss and gain;
But the golden sunlight warms my home,
    Or on my skylight patters the rain,
    As I paint or sing my castles in Spain.

No checks that smile for a day, and melt,
    The postman brings to my humble door;
But letters from friends whose love is felt
    To be richer than all the golden store
    Of the millionnaire whose soul is poor.

Gold is good, but 't is not the best.
  True love's bank, can it ever break ?
What if it should ?   The sun in the west
  Sinks and rises again, to make
  A long, long banquet of Give and Take.

Time is passing, but time is renewed.
  Life runs over with wealth untold.
Age grows younger in all that is good,
  Reaping the fields where Youth stood cold
  In the drear bare furrows, and dreamed of gold.

What if the light of our matin-prime
  Pales in the storm with a struggling beam ;
One ripe day of life's latter time
  Is worth a hundred of fitful gleam,
  Is worth long years of an aimless dream.

O misty land of uncertain youth,
  Low-lying swamps of fear and doubt !
We have left you below for the heights of truth.
  We have found through the fogs a pathway out.
  Below us the youths and maidens shout,

Wandering, careless, through roads unknown,
  Wrapped in the soft, warm, vapory air.

Here in the clear, still upper zone
  We see how wide is life, how fair,
  While age's light gilds age's care.

What if the snow-wreath crown our heads?
  We gain the electric strength of frost.
We are treading the path each mortal treads.
  We are nearing the spring.   We have counted the cost.
  We trust, ay, know we shall not be lost.

I IN THEE, AND THOU IN ME.

I AM but clay in thy hands, but Thou art the all-loving
  artist.
 Passive I lie in thy sight, yet in my selfhood I strive
So to embody the life and the love thou ever impartest,
 That in my sphere of the finite I may be truly alive.

Knowing thou needest this form, as I thy divine inspiration,
 Knowing thou shapest the clay with a vision and pur-
  pose divine,
So would I answer each touch of thy hand in its loving
  creation,
 That in my conscious life thy power and beauty may
  shine,

Reflecting the noble intent thou hast in forming thy
  creatures ;
 Waking from sense into life of the soul, and the image
  of thee ;

K

Working with thee in thy work to model humanity's
      features
  Into the likeness of God, myself from myself I would
      free.

One with all human existence, no one above or below me ;
  Lit by thy wisdom and love, as roses are steeped in
      the morn ;
Growing from clay to a statue, from statue to flesh, till
      thou know me
  Wrought into manhood celestial, and in thine image
      re-born.

So in thy love will I trust, bringing me sooner or later
  Past the dark screen that divides these shows of the
      finite from thee.
Thine, thine only, this warm dear life, O loving Creator !
  Thine the invisible future, born of the present, must be.

TO THE MEMORY OF MARGARET FULLER OSSOLI.

ODE READ AT THE CELEBRATION OF HER BIRTHDAY BY THE
NEW ENGLAND WOMEN'S CLUB, BOSTON, MAY 23, 1870.

I.

LIFE'S rearward vistas slowly close behind,
And evermore recede, the glare and shade
Blending in neutral tints far down the glade
   Where youth stepped unconfined,
Or bounded upwards, light and undismayed,
Or struggled through the underbrush and thorns,
Baffled and mad to hear the winding horns
So far away triumphant on the heights
Where some found truth, some error's foggy breath,
   And some fame's evanescent lights,
Or desolate old age, or crown of early death.

II.

   Dim in the distance fade
   The sunshine and the shade ;

And many a light that blazed and shone,
Into the horizon's mist has gone.
One record rises from our past,
That shall forever last ;
A name our age can never
From its remembrance sever.
We bear it in our hearts to-day,
Fresh as the perfume of the May.
It vibrates in the air, a rich, full-chorded strain
Touched with weird minor moods of pain,
The music of a life revealed to few,
Till to the age Death gave the fame long due,
And made the unfinished symphony a part
Of the great growing century's mind and heart.

III.

But when I strive the music to rehearse,
How feebly rings my verse !
And why intone this melody of rhyme
For one, the noblest woman of her time,
Whose soul, a pure and radiant chrysolite,
Dims the superfluous arts our social forms invite ?

Yet she whose ear so well could understand
The singer's meaning, though unskilled the hand

That swept the imperfect chords
Responsive to his words,
Would not disdain the slenderest song he brings,
Nor slight the impulse of the earnest strings.
So, while we gather here,
Fain would I bring some offering sincere
Though small,— a flower or two,
Pale amaranth, wild rose, or harebell blue,
Or throw at least a chaplet on her bier.

IV.

While others stood aloof and smiled in scorn
Of one to new and noble effort born ;
Or from tame rounds of fashion and of wealth
Turned, glancing back by stealth,
And wondered, then but slowly, faintly praised
The exuberant soul that dared to flash and soar
Beyond the petty bounds
Of their trim garden grounds, —
She with wise intuition raised
Her image of ideal womanhood,
The incarnate True and Fair and Good,
Set in a light but seldom seen before.
While with the early watchers in the dawn
Of intellectual faith her hopeful eyes,

Patiently waiting, from the crowd withdrawn,
　　She saw a newer morning rise
　And flame from cloud to cloud, and climb
　Across the dreary tracts of time.
The garnered wisdom of the past she drew
Into her life, as flowers the sun and dew;
　　Yet valued all her varied lore
　　But as the avenue and door
　　That opened to the Primal Beam
　　　And sense of Truth supreme.

　And so beyond her earlier bounds she grew, —
　All the quaint essences from study gained
　Fused in a human fellowship anew;
While that too conscious life, in younger years o'erstrained,
　Of long, deep, lonely introversion born,
　　　Distilled like dews of morn,
And dropped on high and low the blessing it contained.
　Her glowing pen through many a thoughtful page
　Discoursed in subtle questions of the age,
　Or glanced in lighter mood at themes less grave,
　The brilliant glitter of a summer wave.
　Her sweet persuasive voice we still can hear
　Ruling her charméd circle like a queen;
　While wit and fancy sparkled ever clear

Her graver moods between.
The pure perennial heat
Of youth's ideal love forever glowed
Through all her thoughts and words, and overflowed
The listeners round her seat.

So, like some fine-strung golden harp,
Tuned by many a twist and warp
Of discipline and patient toil,
And oft disheartening recoil, —
Attuned to highest and to humblest use, —
All her large heroic nature
Grew to its harmonious stature.
Nor any allotted service did refuse,
While those around her but half understood
How wise she was, how good,
How nobly self-denying, as she tasked
Heart, mind, and strength for truth, nor nobler office asked.

V.

Nor honor less, nor praise
To her whose later days
Were pledged to lift wronged Justice to her seat.
And though Rome's new-lit torch
Blew backward, but to scorch

The hand that held it, dropping at her feet,
Quenched in the patriots' blood, not incomplete
Her task, though all the heroic strains she sang
To chronicle a struggling nation's pang —
    The records of the strife
    That agonized its life —
Were strewn upon the wind like withered flowers,
And gulfed in roaring floods, — Italia's loss, and ours!

Alas! how could we with our lamp of hope
Read thy perplexed and darkened horoscope?
How could we know, when Destiny's great loom
Thy life's most precious threads inwove
With all love's rich embroidery of love,
    That its bright tissue held the shade
    Of death across the golden braid, —
The inevitable woof of death and tragic doom!
        When ties were sweetest, dearest;
        When love, when hope, were nearest;
        When eyes grew bright to greet thee;
        When arms were stretched to meet thee;
        When all thy life was flowering
            As in a garden home, —
        The storm beyond was lowering,
            The end of all was come!

I seem to hear
The grand, sweet music of that earnest life,
Grander and sweeter in its later strife,
Stop, suddenly drowned amid the tempest drear.
I hear that harp whose strings,
Whose delicate, thoughtful strings should well have played
Some hopeful melody of woods and springs;
Some high heroic march
Beneath a Roman arch;
Some lofty strain that made
The soul flush to its sharing
The soldier's toil and daring, —
Swept, like a wind-harp to wild agony
By bitter winds of destiny;
Then, musical no more,
Dead, mute, and shattered on the lonely shore!

VI.

Had fate accorded with love's passionate prayer;
Had she lived on with us, with us grown old,
Through war, through peace, through present toil and care,
Through future progress; could she now behold
The triumph of the land,
Standing where now we stand, —

8

The nation saved from brute Rebellion's strife,
And pledged to live a newer, healthier life;
   Had she but seen our wider range,
   The splendor of our coming lights,
Her vision and her strength grown with her change
     From lonely days and nights,
To all that woman needs to make complete
     In wifehood and maternal ties
The ripened mind and heart, — a union sweet,
     Tender and strong and wise.

     But ah !   Fate suffered not,
     Nor stayed her hasting feet.
     No record but a blot,
     A cherished leaf or two
     Of tender love and true, —
No other relic sad and sweet
     The cruel sea gave back
     From out the storm and wrack,
     From out the billows wild.
     Only one little child
     The weeping sailors bore
     And buried on that shore, —
All that the ocean left of thine and thee,
O friend, whom we again shall never see !

VII.

Where now, where,
O spirit pure, where walk those shining feet ?
Whither, in groves beyond the treacherous seas,
Beyond our sense of time, divinely, dimly fair,
Brighter than gardens of Hesperides, —
Whither dost thou move on, complete
 And beauteous, ringed around
 In mystery profound,
 By gracious companies who share
 That strange, supernal air !
Or art thou sleeping dreamless, knowing naught
 Of good or ill, of life or death ?
Or art thou but a breeze of Heaven's breath,
 A portion of all life, inwrought
In the eternal essence ? — All in vain,
 Tangled in misty webs of time,
 Out on the undiscovered clime
 Our clouded eyes we strain.
 We cannot pierce the veil.
 As the proud eagles fail
 Upon their upward track,
 And flutter gasping back
From the thin empyrean, so with wing
 Baffled and humbled, we but guess

All we shall gain, by all the soul's distress,
All we shall be, by our poor worthiness.
    And so we write and sing
Our dreams of time and space, and call them — heaven.
    We only know that all is for the best ;
        To God we leave the rest.

    So, reverent beneath the mystery
        Of life and death, we yield
    Back to the great Unknown the spirit given
    A few brief years to blossom in our field.
        Nor shall time's all-devouring sea
        Despoil this brightest century
    Of all thou hast been, and shalt ever be.
        The age shall guard thy fame,
        And reverence thy name.
There is no cloud on them.   There is no death for thee !

IAPIS.

" Phœbo ante alios dilectus, Iapis
Iasides : acri quondam cui captus amore
Ipse suas artes, sua munera, lætus Apollo
Augurium, citharamque, dabat, celeresque sagittas.
Ille, ut depositi proferret fata parentis,
Scire potestates herbarum, usumque medendi,
Maluit, et mutas agitare inglorius artes."

VIRGIL, *Æneid*, B. XII.

IN Troas, on Mount Ida's sloping side,
There lived a shepherd youth whom Phœbus loved,
Iapis, old Iasius' son, his name.
His father, feeble, agéd, many a month
Had kept his couch, or basking in the sun
Sat, mid the mossy rocks that faced the south,
Before his cottage door.   Long had his son,
His sole attendant, striven to bring back
His father's failing strength ; but they were poor,
And in all arts medicinal unskilled.
Yet all was done that filial love and care,
Unschooled in lore of herbs and cures, could do.

On Ida's slopes, one night, the stifled winds
Of summer had all fainted in the heats
That pressed upon the bosoms of the hills,
But rose again, with crashing bursts of storm,
And sweeping rains, that drenched the piny clefts;
And through the incumbent night in blazing spasms
Flashed far and fast the thunderbolts of Jove;
A beautiful and blinding light, that all
The landscape, and the distant towers of Troy,
And the gray sea away by Tenedos
Seemed dashed with sudden shocks of moonlight mixed
With chaos and the black of Erebus.

Iapis and Iasius sat beneath
Their humble roof, and from the casement gazed
Upon the sky, with long-suspended breath
Between the ominous intervals of fire
And thunder, till at length Iapis spoke.
" Father, it is the anger of the gods,
On us perchance; perchance on Priam's walls
Some overwhelming doom must fall erelong."
But old Iasius answered : " Nay, not so.
My strength ebbs back, as if a weight of years
Rolled from my shoulders.   Though I am no seer,
I feel the presence of the Olympian will,

Masking benignity in portents fierce,
To work some issue, all unknown, yet bright
For thee, for me, and for the Trojan realm.
Lo, now the thunder rolls away; the rain
Has ceased; and only down the mountain gorge
The torrents leap in tumbling cataracts.
The clouds have parted, and the sleepy storm
Flutters his dying fire-wings far away,
Quivering through domes and pinnacles of cloud,
Where on the horizon ride the tossing ships,
Black-masted, heaving with the ocean's swell.
I too would rest. Sleep falls, as not for months,
Upon my weary eyes. Thou too, my son,
More hopefully go seek thy couch. Some good
The gods design, else why this wondrous calm?"

At dawn of day Iapis woke. His sire
Already was awake, a peaceful smile
Upon his lips. "A happy dream I 've had,"
He said, — "a dream of radiant morn and youth.
Golden Apollo mingled with my trance,
And lit with splendor each fantastic shape
That flitted through its changes. Nay, not now,
I will not tell it now, — some day, some morn,
When thou, poor shepherd boy, shalt need no more

Thy mountain goats, thy staff, and humble garb,
And sorry penance and routine of care,
Linked to the fortunes of thy tottering sire.
Apollo, lo, Apollo loves thee, boy !
Go forth this morn, this very morn, and build
An altar to the god in yonder grove.
With hallowed rites and willing sacrifice
Pray to the god of wisdom and of light."

Then forth into the ambrosial air of morn
Iapis went, much pondering in his mind
What dream it may have been that cheered his sire.
It was a morning that seemed all distilled
Of amber, gold and gems, and dewy scents
From fields and woods, the rhyme of heaven with earth.
Pale in the pearly west the white moon hung
Like an inverted silver cup drained dry,
After some midnight banquet of the gods
Withdrawn into the blue, with all their stars.
Beyond the windows to the east uprose
A grove of cedars, dark against the dawn.
Beneath the shadows of the antique boughs
The spicy odors of the night still lay
Entangled in the embraces of the dew.
And o'er the cedars flamed the rose and gold

Of braided clouds fantastically curled,
Dappled and flecked and streaked with opal tints ;
And all the east was ringing with the choirs
Of rapturous birds.   So far away it seemed
From storms and sorrows and all earthly cares,
As though 't were but a step from Ida's top
Into the Olympian calm of deathless gods.

Then down the eastern slope Iapis stepped,
Till the dense cedars, opening, half disclosed,
Through branches interlaced, the imperial morn
That burned from amber-gray to crimson-gold, —
The coming presence of the god of light.
Then, as Iapis thought to grasp his bow
And arrows, and to slay a tawny wolf,
As offered victim at Apollo's shrine,
(So had the youth been taught by custom old)
Sudden uprose the sun ; and in the sun
A face, whose beauty thrilled him with strange awe.
And whether he were sleeping or awake,
He knew not ; yet these words into his soul
Passed, with the rapture of the rising sun :
" Iapis, not from thee do I require
The death of aught, though 't were a prowling wolf
About thy sheepfold.   Sacrifice to me

Is naught, when true devotion such as thine
I know, and know thy depths of love untold.
Fair youth, long, long have I from heights serene
Yearned for communion with the soul enshrined
Within thy mortal frame.   Now have I come
To offer thee the gifts a god alone
Can give.   Lo, here thou liv'st a shepherd's life,
Obscure, inglorious, far from men and towns,
Far from the toils and fame of mighty men
Whose words shake kingdoms, or whose daring hands
O'erthrow the embattled masonry of time;
Or who, with wisdom half allied to us,
Invert the future; or who sweep the lyre,
And chant the strains that live from age to age, —
Our favorites, yet no dearer to our soul
Than thou.   These, for the love I bear, O youth,
These gifts, Apollo's gifts, if thou but choose,
Are thine, thou consecrate alone to me! "

With head bowed down and with a faltering tongue,
As one o'erburdened with a weight of love
He not deserves, or one who cannot gauge
With customary measuring-wand the depths
Of knowledge hidden, hidden yet desired,
And though desired, so hard to be attained;

Not all contented with his present lot,
Yet fearing somewhat the steep, slippery heights
Trod by the shining heroes of his dreams,
Iapis thus replied : " O thou who rul'st
The sun, the day, the march of year on year !
O Fount of light, whom with my simple vows
In rustic fashion every morn I adore!
I am unworthy to accept such gifts.
I know not what they are, I can but guess
Their grandeur; seek some fitter man than me."

He paused.   Again the golden Presence spoke :
" To plead in senates, to enchain the crowd
With words of magic eloquence, to know
The impenetrable future, to ensnare
The secrets of all depths and heights of power,
To wing the arrow from the sounding bow
With fatal aim, to know the muse divine,
And thrill the world with poesy and song, —
Think well, these gifts are thine, if thou but choose ;
For I do love thee better than thou know'st."

So radiant was the sun-god's smile, as thus
He spoke, so winning were his tones, so near
He seemed to come, it was as though some friend

Of half-remembered form, met in a dream,
Held speech with him in sympathetic tones.

Then said Iapis, — for he had pondered long,
And thought upon his hoary-headed sire,—
" O great Apollo, thou hast left unnamed
One gift of thine, — one power that I would prize
O'er all the rest that thou hast offered me.
I have a father, suffering, bent with age,
And he is dear to me, as I to him.
Grant, if it be thy will, most mighty one,
Grant me the knowledge of these herbs that grow
About my feet and in the mountain-clefts,
To know their essence, and extract the cures
That lurk within their leaves and flowers and roots,
And how and when with art medicinal
To use — so I may make e'en poison serve
The ends of restoration — every plant
That suns itself beneath thy sovereign eye.
Thus to my failing sire shall I bring back
His youth and health, and so rejoice with him.
Thus too shall I amid our cities serve
My countrymen, should war or fell disease
Besiege their walls, and know life's noblest use,
To help my fellow-men."

Then Phœbus smiled
With light so radiantly sweet, the youth
Saw how each little flower and mountain weed
Turned to the sun-god; while such fragrance filled
The morn, as never save in heaven is known,
When all the gods are at their ambrosial feasts.

And so Iapis knew his prayer was heard,
And joyful to his hut returned, and told
All to his sire. " Lo now," Iasius said,
" My dream comes. true ; but other than I dreamed.
Riches, and power, and hidden lore, and skill
In augury and archery and the lute
And poet's pen, — all these my fancy found
For thee in vision, but no power to know
The virtues of the commonest weed that grows,
To use the seeming useless, and so heal
And save from pain and death thy fellow-men.
For what would it avail, though thou shouldst stand
A trained familiar at the awful doors
Of life and death and miracle and fate,
Knowing the things that God alone should know ?
Or what to wing the viewless shaft of death,
Destroying, where thy hand should save and bless ?
Or say that thou shouldst own the higher gifts

Of eloquence and poesy and song ?
Better than poet's dreams and singer's tones,
The task to win the secrets wrapped and hid
In Nature's mute and unresponsive breast,
Whose powers unlocked by thought shall lift the race
Of man to endless happiness and strength.
Who toils for fame and power may slip and fall
And crumble to a puff of worthless dust;
Who lives to help his kind, how mean soe'er
His lot may be, deserves, not love alone
Of all the immortals, but a fellowship
With them shall win, that honors Jove himself."

THE WORKSHOP AND THE BRONZE.

THE heaving bellows pants no more,
    The fiery forge is cold and still,
Wide open stands the furnace door,
    The ashes on the hearth are chill;
The noise, the labor, and the heat are o'er.

The pale light of the waning day
    Through dim and smoky windows falls,
And gleams with melancholy gray
    On scattered tools and blackened walls;
The weary workmen all have gone away.

But on a pedestal, behold,
    There stands a statue of a man, —
A bronze as perfect-pure as gold, —
    Completion of the artist's plan,
Shaped in the heat, consummate from the mould.

O thou through toil and furnace-fires
　　Purged of the dross that marred thy youth,
And moulded to divine desires
　　By master-hands of love and truth,
Till all thy being to the Best aspires, —

　　Thy earthly house that saw thy prime
　　　Alive with busy thought and hand
　　May empty lie.　But thou sublime
　　　Shalt in thy soul's fair image stand,
And smile at fate and all the change of time.

THE EVENING PRIMROSE.

"WHAT are you looking at?" the farmer said;
  "That's nothing but a yellow flowering weed."
We turned, and saw our neighbor's grizzled head
  Above the fence, but took of him no heed.

There stood the simple man, and wondered much
  At us, who wondered at the twilight flowers
Bursting to life, as if a spirit's touch
  Awoke their slumbering souls to answer ours.

"It grows all o'er the island, wild," said he;
  "There are plenty in my field : I root 'em out.
But, for my life, it puzzles me to see
  What you make such a wonderment about."

The good man turned and to his supper went;
  While, kneeling on the grass with mute delight

Or whispered words, around the plant we bent,
　　To watch the opening buds that love the night.

Slowly the rosy dusk of eve departed,
　　And one by one the pale stars bloomed on high;
And one by one each folded calyx started,
　　And bared its golden petals to the sky.

One throb from star to flower seemed pulsing through
　　The night, — one living spirit blending all
In beauty and in mystery ever new, —
　　One harmony divine through great and small.

E'en our plain neighbor, as he sips his tea,
　　I doubt not, through his window feels the sky
Of evening bring a sweet and tender plea
　　That links him even to dreamers such as I.

So through the symbol-alphabet that glows
　　Through all creation, higher still and higher
The spirit builds its faith, and ever grows
　　Beyond the rude form of its first desire.

O boundless Beauty and Beneficence!
　　O deathless Soul that breathest in the weeds

And in a starlit sky ! — e'en through the rents
  Of accident thou serv'st all human needs ;

Nor stoopest idly to our petty cares ;
  Nor knowest great or small, since folded in
By universal Love, all being shares
  The life that ever shall be or hath been.

October 10, 1872.

IN A CHURCH.

I.

THE organ breathed in harmonies so sweet,
   That Paradise, with sons of light and air,
And daughters of the morn, seemed floating round :
   Rich modulations, vaulting fugues that bear
The heart a captive ; as when Ganymede
   Borne by Jove's eagle to the Olympian feast,
Sees the earth fade, and all the sky becomes
   Before his gaze one wide auroral east.

II.

The sunshine, flashing through the flying cloud,
   Struck on the many-tinted window-panes,
And dashed a chord of colors on the wall,
   Now strong, now fading like the dying strains, —
A prismy gush of hues that slid oblique
   Down the gray columns, like a glowing truth
Whose white light tinted in a poet's brain
   Breaks in a thousand rhymes of love and youth.

III.

The hour was framed for silent thought and prayer,
　The place should seem a heavenly shepherd's fold.
We waited for a voice that might sustain

　Our spirits' flight, nor let the air grow cold
About our wings, but bear us higher still,

　Till touched by faith and love and wisdom pure,
We felt the power that lifted man to God, —

　The central truths no dogmas could obscure.

IV.

And yet the priest, discordant mid accords,
　With waste of words, half truth, half error mixed,
Thin homilies and theologic prayers, —

　He only jarred the music, spread betwixt
Nature and God a cloud that dimmed the sun,

　And made the inspiring church a vaulted tomb;
And not till once again we trod the street

　Vanished that shadow of imagined doom.

DECEMBER.

No more the scarlet maples flash and burn
    Their beacon-fires from hilltop and from plain;
The meadow-grasses and the woodland fern
    In the bleak woods lie withered once again.

The trees stand bare, and bare each stony scar
    Upon the cliffs; half frozen glide the rills;
The steel-blue river like a scimitar
    Lies cold and curved between the dusky hills.

Over the upland farm I take my walk,
    And miss the flaunting flocks of golden-rod;
Each autumn flower a dry and leafless stalk,
    Each mossy field a track of frozen sod.

I hear no more the robin's summer song
    Through the gray network of the wintry woods;
Only the cawing crows that all day long
    Clamor about the windy solitudes.

Like agate stones upon earth's frozen breast,
  The little pools of ice lie round and still ;
While sullen clouds shut downward east and west
  In marble ridges stretched from hill to hill.

Come once again, O southern wind, — once more
  Come with thy wet wings flapping at my pane ;
Ere snow-drifts pile their mounds about my door,
  One parting dream of summer bring again.

Ah, no ! I hear the windows rattle fast ;
  I see the first flakes of the gathering snow,
That dance and whirl before the northern blast.
  No countermand the march of days can know.

December drops no weak, relenting tear,
  By our fond summer sympathies ensnared ;
Nor from the perfect circle of the year
  Can even winter's crystal gems be spared.

  1872.

A CHINESE STORY.

NONE are so wise as they who make pretence
To know what fate conceals from mortal sense.
This moral from a tale of Ho-hang-ho
Might have been drawn a thousand years ago,
Long ere the days of spectacles and lenses,
When men were left to their unaided senses.

Two young short-sighted fellows, Chang and Ching,
Over their chopsticks idly chattering,
Fell to disputing which could see the best.
At last they agreed to put it to the test.
Said Chang, " A marble tablet, so I hear,
Is placed upon the Bo-hee temple near,
With an inscription on it.   Let us go
And read it (since you boast your optics so),
Standing together at a certain place
In front, where we the letters just may trace.

Then he who quickest reads the inscription there
The palm for keenest eyes henceforth shall bear."
  "Agreed," said Ching; "and let us try it soon.
Suppose we say to-morrow afternoon."
"Nay, not so soon," said Chang; "I'm bound to go
To-morrow a day's ride from Ho-hang-ho,
And sha'n't be ready till the following day.
At ten A. M. on Thursday, let us say."

So 't was arranged.   But Ching was wide awake.
Time by the forelock he resolved to take;
And to the temple went at once, and read
Upon the tablet, "To the illustrious Dead,
The chief of Mandarins, the great Goh-Bang."
Scarce had he gone, when stealthily came Chang,
Who read the same; but, peering closer, he
Spied in a corner what Ching failed to see, —
The words, "This tablet is erected here
By those to whom the great Goh-Bang was dear."

So, on the appointed day — both innocent
As babes, of course — these honest fellows went
And took their distant station.   And Ching said,
"I can read plainly, 'To the illustrious Dead,
The chief of Mandarins, the great Goh-Bang.'"
"And is that all that you can spell?" said Chang.

9   M

" I see what you have read, but furthermore,
In smaller letters, toward the temple door,
Quite plain, ' This tablet is erected here
By those to whom the great Goh-Bang was dear.' "

" My sharp-eyed friend, there are no such words ! " said
        Ching.
" They 're there," said Chang, " if I see anything,
As clear as daylight ! "   " Patent eyes, indeed,
You have ! " cried Ching. " Do you think I cannot
        read ? "
" Not at this distance, as I can," Chang said ;
" If what you say you saw is all you read."

In fine, they quarrelled, and their wrath increased ;
Till Chang said, " Let us leave it to the priest.
Lo, here he comes to meet us."   " It is well,"
Said honest Ching ; " no falsehood he will tell."

The good man heard their artless story through,
And said, " I think, dear sirs, there must be few
Blest with such wondrous eyes as those you wear.
There 's no such tablet or inscription there.
There was one, it is true ; 't was moved away
And placed *within* the temple yesterday."

A SONG OF HOME.

I.

HERE we are once more together
    Where we parted long ago :
Father, mother, sisters, brothers ;
    Hearts and faces all aglow.
Rain is on the roof above us,
    But no cloud can chill our joys
Round the old familiar table,
    As we sat when girls and boys.
            What care we for wind and rain ?
            We are all at home again.

II.

Here still hang the dear old pictures,
    And the old books we used to share ;
Here 's the old arm-chair in the corner,
    And the old clock upon the stair ;

There the roses at the window
  Tossing up against the pane,
And the old pear-tree in the garden,
  And the lilacs in the lane.
      What care we for wind and rain?
      We are all at home again.

III.

O, the weary days we 've wandered
  Vanish in the fireside's glow;
And the happy hours of childhood
  Glimmer back from long ago.
Storms may beat upon our dwelling.
  Light the lamps of love and home.
We are all once more together,
  Never, never more to roam.
      What care we for wind and rain?
      We are all at home again.

A SPRING-GROWL.

—◆—

I.

WOULD you think it? Spring is come.
Winter's paid his passage home ;
Packed his ice-box, — gone — half-way
To the Arctic Pole, they say.
But I know the old ruffian still
Skulks about from hill to hill,
Where his freezing footprints cling,
               Though 't is Spring ?

II.

Heed not what the poets sing
In their rhymes about the Spring.
Spring was once a potent queen,
Robed in blossoms and in green.
That, I think, was long ago.
Is she buried in the snow,
Deaf to all our carolling, —
               Poor old Spring ?

III.

Windows rattling in the night ;
Shutters that you thought were tight
Slamming back against the wall ;
Ghosts of burglars in the hall ;
Roaring winds and groaning trees ;
Chimneys shuddering in the breeze ;
Doleful dumps in everything, —
        Such is Spring.

IV.

Sunshine trying hard awhile
On the bare brown fields to smile ;
Frozen ruts and slippery walks ;
Gray old crops of last year's stalks ;
Shivering hens and moping cows ;
Curdled sap in leafless boughs
Nipped by Winter's icy sting, —
        Such is Spring.

V.

Yet the other day I heard
Something that I thought a bird.
He was brave to come so soon ;
But his pipes were out of tune,

And he chirped as if each note
Came from flannels round his throat,
And he had no heart to sing, —
   Ah, poor thing !

VI.

If there comes a little thaw,
Still the air is chill and raw.
Here and there a patch of snow,
Dirtier than the ground below,
Dribbles down a marshy flood ;
Ankle-deep you stick in mud
In the meadows, — while you sing,
   " This is Spring."

VII.

Are there violets in the sod,
Crocuses beneath the clod ?
When will Boreas give us peace ?
Or has Winter signed a lease
For another month of frost,
Leaving Spring to pay the cost ?
For it seems he still is king,
   Though 't is Spring.

STATEN ISLAND, March 26, 1873.

WAITING BY THE SEA.

———◆———

ALONE upon the windy hills
    I stand and face the open sea,
And drink the southern breeze which fills
    The sails that bring my love to me.

Far out the shores and woodlands reach,
    Till lost in mists of pearly gray,
Or crossed by lines of yellow beach,
    And flashing breakers far away.

Alone upon the windy slopes
    I watch the long blue level wall
Of ocean, where my wingéd hopes
    Like fluttering sea-birds fly and call.

O happy pilot-boats that dance
  Across the sparkling miles of sea !
O greet her, should ye hail by chance
  The ship that bears my love to me !

And does she lean upon the deck
  And strain her eyes till land appears,
As I to catch the white-winged speck
  That clears away my gathering fears ?

By long low beach and wooded crag
  The crowded sails go glimmering past ;
But none that bear the well-known flag
  And pennon streaming from the mast.

O ocean, wrinkling in the sun !
  O breeze that blowest from the sea !
Waft into port, ere day is done,
  My love, my life, again to me !

She comes, she comes ! I see the sails
  Like rounded sea-shells full and white.
I hear the booming gun that hails
  The coming of my heart's delight.

9 *

I hear the sailors' distant song ;
   They crowd the deck in bustling glee ;
And there is one amid the throng
   Who waves a rosy scarf to me.

The sun has set ; the air is still ;
   The twilight reddens o'er the sea ;
The full moon rises o'er the hill ;
   But joy like sunrise shines for me.

1873.

SHELLING PEAS.

A PASTORAL.

No, Tom, you may banter as much as you please;
But it 's all the result of the shellin' them peas.
Why, I had n't the slightest idea, do you know,
That so serious a matter would out of it grow.
I tell you what, Tom, I do feel kind o' scared.
I dreamed it, I hoped it, but never once dared
To breathe it to her.   And besides, I must say
I always half fancied *she* fancied Jim Wray.
So I felt kind o' stuffy and proud, and took care
To be out o' the way when that feller was there
A danglin' around; for thinks I, if it 's him
That Katy likes best, what 's the use lookin' grim
At Katy or Jim, — for it 's all up with me;
And I 'd better jest let 'em alone, do you see?
But you would n't have thought it; that girl never keered
The snap of a pea-pod for Jim's bushy beard.
Well, here 's how it was.   I was takin' some berries

Across near her garden, to leave at Aunt Mary's ;
When, jest as I come to the old elhum-tree,
All alone in the shade, that June mornin', was she —
Shellin' peas — setting there on a garden settee.
I swan, she was handsomer 'n ever I seen,
Like a rose all alone in a moss-work o' green.
Well, there was n't no use ; so, says I, I 'll jest linger
And gaze at her here, hid behind a syringa.
But she heard me a movin', and looked a bit frightened.
So I come and stood near her.   I fancied she brightened
And seemed sort o' pleased.   So I hoped she was well ;
And — would she allow me to help her to shell ?
For she sot with a monstrous big dish full of peas
Jest fresh from the vines, which she held on her knees.
"May I help you, Miss Katy ? " says I. "As you please,
Mr. Baxter," says she.   "But you 're busy, I guess " —
Glancin' down at my berries, and then at her dress.
" Not the least.   There 's no hurry.   It ain't very late ;
And I 'd rather be here, and Aunt Mary can wait."
So I sot down beside her ; an' as nobody seen us,
I jest took the dish, and I held it between us.
And I thought to myself I must make an endeavor
To know which she likes, Jim or me, now or never !
But I could n't say nothin'.   We sot there and held
That green pile between us.   She shelled, and I shelled ;

And *pop* went the pods; and I could n't help thinkin'
Of popping the question.   A kind of a sinkin'
Come over my spirits; till at last I got out,
" Mister Wray 's an admirer of yours, I 've no doubt
You see him quite often."   " Well, sometimes.   But why
And what if I did ? "   " O, well, nothin'," says I.
" Some folks says you 're goin' to marry him, though."
" Who says so ? " says she; and she flared up like tow
When you throw in a match.   " Well, some folks that I
       know."
" 'T ain't true, sir," says she.   And she snapped a big pod,
Till the peas, right and left, flew all over the sod.
Then I looked in her eyes, but she only looked down
With a blush that she tried to chase off with a frown.
" Then it 's somebody else you like better," says I.
" No, it ain't though," says she; and I thought she
       would cry.
Then I tried to say somethin'; it stuck in my throat,
And all my idees were upset and afloat.
But I said I knew somebody 'd 'loved her so long —
Though he never had told her — with feelin's so strong
He was ready to die at her feet, if she chosed,
If she only could love him ! — I hardly supposed
That she cared for him much, though.   And so, Tom, —
       and so, —

For I thought that I saw how the matter would go, —
With my heart all a jumpin' with rapture, I found
I had taken her hand, and my arm was around
Her waist ere I knew it, and she with her head
On my shoulder, — but no, I won't tell what she said.
The birds sang above us ; our secret was theirs ;
The leaves whispered soft in the wandering airs.
I tell you the world was a new world to me.
I can talk of these things like a book now, you see.
But the peas ? Ah, the peas *in* the pods were a mess
Rather bigger than those that we shelled, you may guess.
It 's risky to set with a girl shellin' peas.
You may tease me now, Tom, just as much as you please.

LOUIS NAPOLEON.

So, he is gone, — the shadow of a name !
Long since we saw the dull, expiring flame
Flare in its socket.   What he was and did
From Europe and the world cannot be hid ;
The crowned adventurer, who set his heel
Upon a people, and with clamps of steel,
Called law and order, fastened deep and broad
A throne sustained by perjury, force, and fraud.

Look back a few short years, and ask what gain,
What boon, to Europe was Napoleon's reign.
" He fought for Italy," you say.   'T is true.
But then he always held himself in view, —
Himself first, France's strength and glory next.
Austria must needs be humbled ; England vexed,
Left playing second, with her eyes askance,
Droning a surly moral bass, while France

Led on the battle orchestra. Her name
Must glow anew with the old chivalric flame;
And he — the man of destiny — the head
Of the new movement. So his armies bled
In Lombardy. He, with his brave Zouaves,
Would do no thing, and least this thing, by halves.
All went like clock-work. France was ever great
In system. But, unluckily, the gate
That led to Venice was too strongly barred.
Yes, as you say, it was a trifle hard
For the orchestral leader to plunge o'er
Those quadrilateral *bars* through smoke and gore;
To see his brave men — those swift living notes
In his heroic symphony — their coats
Stained deep in Solferino's dust and blood,
Marshalled again to serve as naught but food
For powder, — faces gashed and burnt and blurred
By bayonet, ball, and fever. So the word
Was given to change the programme; for the war
Was swelling to a size too great by far,
Involving interests which were not " France."
Further he would not, could not now advance,
Though Freedom stood dismayed. A treaty straight
Was signed, before the act should be too late:
Sardinia keeping all that she had won;

But Venice, pining for the air and sun,
And stretched upon her Austrian dungeon-floor,
Must needs be left bound closer than before.
Hard, when her prison was about to ope,
To bolt it in her face, to kill her hope !
But France, and Europe, and that blessed fiction,
" Balance of power," had wrought more cool conviction.

So Villafranca's treaty closed the lid
Of the Pandora-box, and Hope was left ;
And what the lion failed in, the fox did.
For Francis Joseph must have been bereft
Of brains, to be outwitted there and then, —
His sails struck windless by a stroke o' the pen ;
His long-famed cunning all outdone and shamed,
That he consented to a treaty framed
Purposely vague, to favor Italy,
Leaving an open door he did not see.
" Bring the Dukes back," forsooth ; but nothing said,
Should the good people choose to rule instead.
This credit then he takes, — Napoleon
Suffered the Revolution to move on ;
He could not interfere to keep the kings
When the unfettered countries spread their wings.
Prudently stood aside, when down the slope

The great machine rolled, freighted with the hope
Of nations who with shouts of joy beheld
(By nature's law of gravity impelled)
The car of state, so long a stranded thing
On lonely heights, the plaything of a king,
Now move on common roads where brethren meet
In friendly intercourse and converse sweet.
But never with a finger-tip did he
E'er thrust aside superfluous tyranny.
Enough for him that kings were kings; this fact
Pledged him to keep their right divine intact.

Magician though he was, he raised a ghost
He could not lay, and made this fault a boast;
Built up a throne veneered and varnished well
With democratic gloss, a glittering shell
That feared the people's touch, and ill could bear
The slightest breeze of Freedom's common air;
While he who filched the empire, like a thief,
Proclaimed himself the nation's chosen chief.

Imperial author, writing special pleas
For liberal tyranny and a conquered peace, —
Himself his only judge, he from their nooks
Drove out the critic rats that gnawed his books.

Long-armed policeman, smothering Freedom's fires;
Spider-like sitting in a web of wires
Netting all Europe from his central ring;
Throttling the editorial gnats whose sting
Or buzz protests against the bands that wind
The despot's cobwebs round the free-born mind;
Yet loudly boasting that his power relies
Upon the votes of his dear tangled flies.

How long he sat, — this Cæsar of the stage,
This bold, pretending patron of the age!
Muzzled the press, yet bade the people think;
Knelt to the Pope, but gave the crowd a wink;
Now capped a Cardinal, now endowed a school;
Permitted suffrage, under iron rule;
Gave wings to trade, but clogged all daring thought,
Counting all counsel but his own as naught;
Put new wine in old bottles, best in worst,
And clamped them round with iron, lest they burst;
Forced two extremes to marry, last with first;
Wed light to darkness, and misnamed the brood
Born of the union, France's highest good.

Professing friendship for our western main,
He hoped to split our continent in twain;

And while our back is turned to grasp our foe,
Drives in an Austrian wedge at Mexico;
Finds he has bungled sadly, and would fain
Withdraw poor Maximilian again.
Would like to recall his forces too from Rome,
But fears the hubbub of his priests at home.
So, pledged to God and Mammon, he prolongs
The strife with chaos, smiles on rights and wrongs;
The Pope's *non possumus* most blandly hears,
And leaves poor Rome in misery and in tears;
Prates loud of nations' rights, and ten times o'er
Opens and shuts a people's prison-door.

Now, time brings round its retributions strange.
O'er Europe's face there sweeps a mighty change.
Now Germany compact and bristling stands
Guarding her blue Rhine from the invader's hands.
Now Venice sets her sea-pearl in the ring
Worn by young Italy's victorious king.
Now Rome, e'en Rome, must add her eternal fame
To a throne upborne by Garibaldi's name;
Unguarded by her Gallic sentinel,
She loosely holds the keys of heaven and hell;
Her Pope, whose thunders rattled west and east,
Changed by a pen-scrawl to a harmless priest.

And he, the mighty Emperor, whose word
Held Europe spell-bound, in war's thunders heard
A voice that overruled his subtile tricks,
His blunders and his shuffling politics,
His sham democracy, his hard decrees,
His double-dealings and diplomacies.
These brought their sure results, — ambition checked,
A tarnished splendor, and an empire wrecked,
And that distrust through every heart that crept,
At rights withheld and promises unkept ;
While downward sank his star, unmourned of all
Who hail the nation's rise, the usurper's fall ;
Till death has swept away the last frail chance
That cheered the friends of tyranny in France.

BY THE SHORE OF THE RIVER.

THROUGH the gray willows the bleak winds are raving
    Here on the shore with its driftwood and sands.
Over the river the lilies are waving,
    Bathed in the sunshine of Orient lands.
    Over the river, the wide, dark river,
    Spring-time and summer are blooming forever.

Here all alone on the rocks I am sitting,
    Sitting and waiting, — my comrades all gone, —
Shadows of mystery drearily flitting
    Over the surf with its sorrowful moan, —
    Over the river, the strange, cold river.
    Ah, must I wait for the boatman forever?

Wife and children and friends were around me;
    Labor and rest were as wings to my soul;

Honor and love were the laurels that crowned me ;
    Little I recked how the dark waters roll.
    But the deep river, the gray misty river,
    All that I lived for has taken forever.

Silently came a black boat o'er the billows ;
    Stealthily grated the keel on the sand ;
Rustling footsteps were heard through the willows ;
    There the dark boatman stood waving his hand,
    Whispering, " I come, — from the shadowy river ;
    She who is dearest must leave thee forever ! "

Suns that were brightest and skies that were bluest
    Darkened and paled in the message he bore.
Year after year went the fondest, the truest,
    Following that beckoning hand to the shore.
    Down to the river, the cold, grim river,
    Over whose waters they vanished forever.

Yet not in visions of grief have I wandered ;
    Still have I toiled, though my ardors have flown.
Labor is manhood ; and life is but squandered
    Dreaming vague dreams of the future alone.
    Yet from the tides of the mystical river
    Voices of spirits are whispering ever.

Lonely and old, in the dusk I am waiting,
    Till the dark boatman with soft muffled oar
Glides o'er the waves, and I hear the keel grating, —
    See the dim beckoning hand on the shore,
    Wafting me over the welcoming river
    To gardens and homes that are shining forever !

THE AMERICAN PANTHEON.

WHEN Rufus Griswold built his Pantheon wide,
　　And set a hundred poets round its walls,
Did he believe their statues would abide
　　The tests of time upon their pedestals?

A hundred poets!   Some in Parian stone,
　　Perchance; and some in brittle plaster cast;
And some mere busts, whose names are hardly known;—
　　Dii minores of a voiceless past.

Time was when many there so neatly niched
　　Held each within his court a sovereign sway;
Each in his turn his little world enriched,
　　The ephemeral poet-laureate of his day.

Ah, what is fame?   Star after star goes out, —
　　Lost Pleiads in the firmament of truth;
Our kings discrowned ere died the distant shout
　　That hailed the coronation of their youth.

Few are the world's great singers.   Far apart,
    Thrilling with love, yet wrapped in solitude,
They sit communing with the common heart
    That binds the race in human brotherhood.

A wind of heaven o'er their musing breathes,
    And wakes them into verse, — as April turns
The frozen sods to violets, and unsheathes
    The forest flowers amid the leaves and ferns.

And we who dare not wear the immortal crown
    And singing robes, at least may hear and dream,
While strains from prophet lips come floating down ;
    Inspired by them to sing some humbler theme.

Nay, nothing can be lost whose living stems
    Rooted in truth sprang up to beauty's flower.
The spangles of the stage may flout the gems
    On queenly breasts, but only for an hour.

The fashion of the time may claim its own ;
    The soul whose vision custom cannot bar,
The heart that trusts its natural pulse, alone
    Can hope to light the ages, like a star.

O, not for fame the poet of to-day
　Should hunger. Though the world his music scorn,
The after-world may hear, — as mountains gray
　Echo from depths unseen the Alpine horn.

So while around this Pantheon wide I stray,
　Where poets from Freneau to Fay are set,
I doubt not each in turn has sung some lay
　The world will not be willing to forget.

For who in barren rhyme and rhythm could spend
　The costly hours the muse alone should claim,
Did not some finer thought, some nobler end,
　Breathe ardors sweeter than poetic fame?

IN THE FOREST OF FONTAINEBLEAU.

THE lights and shadows of long ago
In the grand old Forest of Fontainebleau
Go with me still wherever I go.

I range my pictures around my room,
Won from the forest's light and gloom ;
Not yet shall they sink to an auction's doom.

They wake me again to the painter's moods ;
They take me back to the wonderful woods,
The wild, dream-haunted solitudes.

They come as Memory waves her wand ;
And I think of the days when with busy hand
I painted alone in the forest grand.

I see the old gnarled oak-trees spread
Their boughs and foliage over my head.
About the mossy rocks I tread.

Under the beeches of Fontainebleau,
In the green dim dells of the Bas-Brëau,
Mid ferns and laurel-tufts I go ;

Or up on the hills, while the woods beneath
Circle me round like a giant-wreath,
Plunge knee-deep in the purple heath ;

Then down to a patch of furzy sand,
Where the white umbrella and easel stand,
And the rocks lie picturesque and grand.

The mellow autumn with fold on fold
Has dressed the woods with a bronzy gold,
And scarlet scarfs of a wealth untold.

The tall gray spotted beeches rise
And seem to touch the unclouded skies,
And round their tops with clamorous cries

The rooks are wheeling to and fro ;
And down on the brown leaf-matting below
The lights and the shadows come and go.

O calm, deep days, when labor moved
With wings of joy to the tasks beloved,
And art its own best guerdon proved !

For such it was, when long ago
I sat in my leafy studio
In the dear old Forest of Fontainebleau.

A DAY OF MEMORIES.

THIS is the road, up through the corn and clover;
    And yonder, the first turning, is the lane.
And that 's the house ; they 've painted it all over,
    So white, I scarce should know the old place again.

Yet the same dear old house.   How well I know it !
    Though changed, and with another face, like me.
'T was here love taught me first to be a poet, —
    Or think I was, the rhyming flowed so free.

Still round the porch the honeysuckles clamber,
    But thicker grown, where hand in hand we stood,
And watched the crimson clouds and sky of amber
    Grow gray and dusk beyond the distant wood.

That was her window.   There I serenaded
    Once in the moonlight of a night in June.
The verses were my own ; I sang unaided,
    Save by my light guitar, my summer tune.

Ah, what warm sonnets did my muse then scatter
     Like wild and golden fruitage from a tree;
And knew that naught I wrote or sang could flatter
     One who outshone all pearls of poesy!

And she was won; and we were pledged forever;
     And yet were parted, — why, I hardly know.
Some fate, but dimly seen, befell to sever
     Two who seemed one so many years ago.

The dear old place! the landscape still unaltered, —
     The stream below, the cedar-trees above;
The same stone-wall and lilacs where I faltered
     The first words, strange and sweet, of boyish love.

Here, up the lane, the broad elms still are growing,
     Each bough unscarred, but larger than of yore.
Yet yonder, where that stranger now is mowing,
     I see they 've felled my favorite sycamore.

How could they do it!   In its shade we parted;
     Or was it wrecked by storm, or lightning blaze?
Like those who kissed their last there, broken-hearted,—
     At least they thought so, in those tender days.

And yonder was a stately beech-tree, slanting
 Across the stream. There once I carved her name.
'T is gone, and flags and water-weeds are flaunting
 Along the brookside, changed, yet still the same.

That parting was like death. But youth 's elastic;
 And hers recovered; so did mine at last.
The world is wide, and human hearts too plastic
 To harden in an unrelenting past.

And far apart her path and mine diverging,
 Each with its separate cares and hopes and dreams,
Long since was stilled young love's tumultuous surging,
 Long since new ties have dimmed those early gleams.

And yet, though wounds will heal, the scars forever
 Cling to the flesh that quivered once, now still;
And there are times when boyhood's pain and fever
 Will wake again with momentary thrill.

So, while I roam about these well-known places,
 Haunted by visions all so sadly sweet,
Those tender tones of old, those mystic graces,
 Seem to prelude the flying of her feet.

10 *   o

Those voices come no more but in my dreaming,
   Too vague to take a shape in uttered words.
Those footsteps in a world remote are gleaming,
   Mine only when I touch the poet's chords.

THE GUEST.

THOU shalt go alone and sad.
  Men will deem thy raptures vain,
And thy products poor and bad,
  And thy progress change, not gain.

When thou meet'st another man,
  Thou from him and he from thee
Shall be shut as by a ban,
  Save in words of courtesy.

Symbols thou shalt deem uncouth
  To his creed are dear and fair;
What to thee is trust and truth
  Seems to him but empty air.

Thou and he are veiled about
  By two webs of time and space,
Spun from films of faith and doubt,
  Warped and woofed across each face.

Only on the central ground
  Paved by character and deeds
Shall the interchange be found
  Spirit touching spirit needs.

If thou strivest much to love
  What the multitude delights,
Thy unwilling guest shall prove
  Darkener of thy own true lights.

In thy home-spun garb and place,
  In the castle of thy thought,
Heed not every stranger face
  Peering in, to tell thee naught.

But when flits a spirit nigh,
  Howsoever mean his state,
If kindred light illumes his eye,
  See that he passes not thy gate.
Him thou shalt house, and entertain,
Till thou hast made his love thy gain.

OCTOBER.

THROUGH golden gates of leaves, through columns gray
Of elms and maples old, whose boughs enlace
In bright cathedral arches overhead,
Enwreathed with scarlet vines ; through bosky tufts
Of underbrush, and willows still so green
Along the hidden brooks, they seem to hold
The summer snared, nor heed the threatening frost,
The calm October days pass one by one,
Smiling in rosy sunsets, ere they flit
Forever from the earth.   How silently
They march, timed to the crickets' ceaseless chirp
Through the still noon, while tall flowers mark their path, —
Blue succory, purple astèrs, golden-rod,
Wild yellow stars, and lonely cardinal-flowers
Whose crimson petals light the sluggish streams.
A clear and wholesome spirit in the air
Touches the earth and all earth's greenest robes

With change so gradual we can feel no loss
Of life, but only mellower, richer hues, —
With music more pathetic, as the wind
Harps through the woods, and red and yellow leaves
Flutter to earth, and whirl in huddled heaps.
So may our little lives, their sap withdrawn,
After their long, still summers, tossed, perchance,
At times, by thunder-gusts or drenched in rains
Of tears, pass peacefully, complete in years
And in that wisdom years alone can bring;
And, having well fulfilled their allotted work,
Sink to their rest, or to their life beyond!

1872.

TO A HALF-FRIEND.

HOW well I know the secret spell to turn
    Your best good-will to me, —
The delicate untruth could I but learn
    Of well-bred flattery.

Just to o'erstep the plain sincerity
    Of friend to friend, no more ;
Only to hint, " Your truth is truth to me,
    No higher and no lower " ;

Seeming to prize your quality and gift,
    Though not on praise intent,
But on the current of our talk to drift
    Into a smooth assent;

To accept without demur or differing eyes
      The half-truth of your thought,
And hide my protest in a compromise
      By dumb good-nature taught;

To linger on your chosen plot of ground,
      As if I too would choose it;
To know a richer realm lies all around
      Your fence, and yet refuse it;

To fear to disagree, though what you say
      Savors of sect and clan;
My fortress of conviction to betray
      And yield life's cherished plan;

To slight the solemn conscience pressing down
      Upon my private faith;
To wear the decorous fashion of the town;
      To hear some shadowy wraith,

Instead of what I know to be myself,
      Utter opinions squared
To social rules, — a poor, unreal elf
      Consenting to be snared,

And playing out a graceful pantomime
    Where earnest words are naught,
To catch the easy plaudits of the time,
    But hide my dearest thought; —

Thus might I win you soon to be my friend,
    Now half a friend at best.
Yet none would say I flattered.   I but send
    Some fractious thoughts to rest.

MUSIC.

READ AT THE ANNUAL DINNER OF THE HARVARD MUSICAL
ASSOCIATION, BOSTON, JANUARY 28, 1874.

WHEN " Music, Heavenly Maid," was *very* young,
She did not sing as poets say she sung.
Unlike the mermaids of the fairy tales,
She paid but slight attention to her scales.
Besides, poor thing ! she had no instruments
But such as rude barbaric art invents.
There were no Steinways then, no Chickerings,
No spinnets, harpsichords, or metal strings ;
No hundred-handed orchestras, no schools
To corset her in contrapuntal rules.
Some rude half-octave of a shepherd's song,
Some childish strumming all the summer long
On sinews stretched across a tortoise-shell,
Such as they say Apollo loved so well ;
Some squeaking flageolet or scrannel pipe,
Some lyre poetic of the banjo type, —
Such were the means she summoned to her aid,
Prized as divine ; on these she sang or played.

Music was then an infant, while she saw
Her sister arts full grown.   Greece stood in awe
Before the Phidian Jove.   Apelles drew
And Zeuxis painted.   Marble temples " grew
As grows the grass " ; and never saw the sun
A statelier vision than the Parthenon.

But she, the Muse who in these latter days
Lifts us and floats us in the golden haze
Of melodies and harmonies divine,
And steeps our souls and senses in such wine
As never Ganymede nor Hebe poured
For gods, when quaffing at the Olympian board, —
She, Heavenly Maid, must ply her music thin,
And sit and thrum her tinkling mandolin,
Chant her rude staves, and only prophesy
Her far-off days of immortality.

E'en so poor Cinderella, when she cowered
Beside her hearth, and saw her sisters, dowered
With grace and wealth, go forth to accomplish all
Their haughty triumphs at the Prince's ball,
While she in russet gown sat mournfully
Singing her " Once a king there chanced to be,"
Yet knows her prince will come ; her splendid days
Are all foreshadowed in her dreaming gaze.

Then, as the years and centuries rolled on,
Like Santa-Clauses they have come and gone,
Bringing all means of utterance to the Muse.
No penny-trumpets, such as children use,
No barbarous Indian drums, no twanging lutes,
No buzzing Jews-harps, no Pandean flutes,
Were stuffed into her stockings, though they hung
On Time's great chimney, as when she was young ;
But every rare and costly instrument
That skill can fabricate or art invent, —
Pianos, organs, viols, horns, trombones,
Hautboys, and clarinets with reedy tones,
Boehm-flutes and cornets, bugles, harps, bassoons,
Huge double-basses, kettle-drum half-moons,
And every queer contrivance made for tunes.

Through these the master-spirits round her throng,
And Europe rings with instruments and song.
Through these she breathes her wondrous symphonies,
Enchanting airs, and choral litanies.
Through these she speaks the word that never dies,
The universal language of the skies.
Around her gather those who held their art
To be of life the dearest, noblest part.
Bach, Handel, Haydn, and Mozart are there ;

Beethoven, chief of all.   The southern air
Is ringing with Rossini's birdlike notes ;
About the north more earnest music floats,
Where Weber, Schumann, Schubert, Mendelssohn,
And long processions of the lords of Tone
All come to attend her.   Like a queen enthroned
She sits and rules the realms she long has owned,
And sways the willing sense, the aspiring soul,
Where thousands bow before her sweet control.

Ah ! greater than all words of mine can say,
The heights, the depths, the glories, of that sway.
No mortal tongue can bring authentic speech
Of that enchanted world beyond its reach ;
No tongue but hers, when, lifted on the waves
Of Tone and Harmony, beyond the graves
Of all we lose, we drift entranced away
Out of the discords of the common day ;
And she, the immortal goddess, on her breast
Lulls us to visions of a sweet unrest,
Smiles at the tyrannies of time and space,
And folds us in a mother's fond embrace,
Till, sailing on upon that mystic sea,
We feel that Life is Immortality.

COMPENSATION.

TEARS wash away the atoms in the eye
    That smarted for a day ;
Rain-clouds that spoiled the splendors of the sky
    The fields with flowers array.

No chamber of pain but has some hidden door
    That promises release ;
No solitude so drear but yields its store
    Of thought and inward peace.

No night so wild but brings the constant sun
    With love and power untold ;
No time so dark but through its woof there run
    Some blessed threads of gold.

And through the long and storm-tost centuries burn
    In changing calm and strife
The Pharos-lights of truth, where'er we turn, —
    The unquenched lamps of life.

O Love supreme! O Providence divine!
    What self-adjusting springs
Of law and life, what even scales, are thine,
    What sure-returning wings

Of hopes and joys that flit like birds away,
    When chilling Autumn blows,
But come again, long ere the buds of May
    Their rosy lips unclose!

What wondrous play of mood and accident
    Through shifting days and years;
What fresh returns of vigor overspent
    In feverish dreams and fears!

What wholesome air of conscience and of thought
    When doubts and forms oppress;
What vistas opening to the gates we sought
    Beyond the wilderness;

Beyond the narrow cells where self-involved,
    Like chrysalids, we wait
The unknown births, the mysteries unsolved
    Of death and change and fate !

O Light divine ! we need no fuller test
    That all is ordered well ;
We know enough to trust that all is best
    Where Love and Wisdom dwell.

    1874.

A BATTLE OF THE ELEMENTS.

THE warring hosts of Winter and of Spring
    Are hurtling o'er the plains.
All night I heard their battle-clarions ring,
    And jar the window-panes.

The arrowy sleet is rattling on the glass ;
    The sky a vault of stone ;
The untimely snows besiege the sprouting grass ;
    The elm-trees toss and moan.

Their swelling buds curl backward as they swing ;
    The crocus in its sheath
Listens, a watchful sentinel, till Spring
    Shall melt the snow's last wreath.

P

The saddened robins flit through leafless trees,
   And chirp with tuneless voice,
And wait the conquering sun, the unbinding breeze;
   They cannot yet rejoice.

Slowly the victor Spring her foe outflanks,
   And countermines his snows;
Then, unawares, along the grassy banks
   Her ambushed violets throws.

Soon she will mask with buds of fragrant white
   Her arsenals of thorns,
And lift her rose-bush banners to the light
   Of soul-entrancing morns.

Along the fields her fairy troops shall hide,
   And conquer by their grace,
And shake their flowery crests, and far and wide
   The surly frosts displace;

Till all the woods are ringing with the glee
   And prophecy of change
That melts the past and sets the present free
   Through Summer's perfect range.

O flagging spring of Honor and of Truth,
  Shalt thou not victor be,
And bring again the faith the nation's youth
  Made one with Liberty ?

Shall the new birth America has known
  Amid her battle-throes
Prove a nipped blossom, blighted ere 't is blown,
  Or a perennial rose ?

April 21, 1874.

MEMORIAL HALL.

AMID the elms that interlace
  Round Harvard's grounds their branches tall,
We greet no walls of statelier grace
  Than thine, our proud Memorial Hall!

Through arching boughs and roofs of green
  Whose dappled lights and shadows lie
Along the turf and road, is seen
  Thy noble form against the sky.

And miles away, on fields and streams,
  Or where the woods the hilltop crown,
The monumental temple gleams,
  A landmark to each neighboring town.

Nor this alone; New England knows
  A deeper meaning in the pride
Whose stately architecture shows
  How Harvard's children fought and died.

Therefore this hallowed pile recalls
   The heroes, young and true and brave,
Who gave their memories to these walls,
   Their lives to fill the soldier's grave.

The farmer, as he drives his team
   To market in the morn, afar
Beholds the golden sunrise gleam
   Upon thee, like a glistening star.

And gazing, he remembers well
   Why stands yon tower so fair and tall.
His sons perhaps in battle fell ;
   For him, too, shines Memorial Hall.

And sometimes as the student glides
   Along the winding Charles, and sees
Across the flats thy glowing sides
   Above the elms and willow-trees,

Upon his oar he 'll turn and pause,
   Remembering the heroic aims
Of those who linked their country's cause
   In deathless glory with their names.

And as against the moonlit sky
    The shadowy mass looms overhead,
Well may we linger with a sigh
    Beneath the tablets of the dead.

The snow-drifts on thy roof shall wreathe
    Their crowns of virgin white for them ;
The whispering winds of summer breathe
    At morn and eve their requiem.

For them the Cambridge bells shall chime
    Across the noises of the town;
The cannon's peal recall their time
    Of stern resolve and brief renown.

Concord and Lexington shall still,
    Like deep to deep, to Harvard call ;
The tall gray shaft on Bunker Hill
    Speak greetings to Memorial Hall.

O, never may the land forget
    Her loyal sons who died that we
Might live, remembering still our debt,
    The costly price of Liberty !

CAMBRIDGE, MASS., April, 1874.

DREAM-LIFE.

"We are such stuff
As dreams are made of, and our little life
Is rounded with a sleep."

LET me be still, lie still and dream again,
And bind the severed links of the golden chain
That glimmered through my morning sleep, but snapped
    When at my door you rapped.

Breakfast? and half past eight? What's that to me?
What's daylight? What are muffins, toast and tea?
"Market, and raining hard, and bills to pay,"
    I think I heard you say.

Ah, yes, this is no dream. I must suppose
There are such things. This is a world of prose.
But I was far away. How real it seemed!
    And yet I only dreamed.

I was a welcome and a happy guest
In a brave palace.   Upward from the west
Long shadows of the lingering afternoon
      In a long day of June

Lay on a lawn.   The palace windows burned
In the red sunset, as I downward turned,
A group of youths and maidens at my side,
      Down to a river wide,

Upon whose waves the western sky lay red.
A barge awaited us; and overhead
Streamed rosy wreaths of cloud.   We sped along,
      With joyous talk and song.

Away, away into a land of light,
Where it was neither morn nor noon nor night,
But dream-light only; and a city stood
      Beyond a tropic wood.

And in the pathway to that happy place
All was incessant change of time and space,
With sudden, sweet surprises, as we went
      In measureless content.

And friends, the absent and the dead, were there ;
And some we never saw, yet seemed to wear
The mingled traits of those we used to know,
  Went passing to and fro

Through festive halls, through gardens strange and rare ;
And all were young, and all were happy there.
How could you wake me from a dream of bliss
  To such a place as this ?

'T was hard to leave that life for one so mean,
For prose and duty and the old routine
Of work. Yet now that I am up and dressed,
  I know that this is best.

The lordly soul is master of its own.
The fair insanities of dreams are flown,
They were but moonlight flashes, broken gleams
  Along its flowing streams.

Another light now shames the tinsel dress
Of drifting fancies wild and rudderless,
Nor can the night's dull jesters now impose
  In Reason's borrowed clothes.

   11 *

And as I plod along, I know that life
Is but the stuff from which with toil and strife
We weave our robe of thought and creed, and tinge
    With dreams its outer fringe.

Work, work, while daylight lasts, and let the night
Spin its thin webs of visionary light,
The rainbow hues that span the cataract
    Of life and living fact!

1874.

THE CENTURY AND THE NATION.

READ BEFORE THE PHI BETA KAPPA SOCIETY OF HARVARD COLLEGE, JUNE 25, 1874.

I.

As when we unbar the windows of the night,
And the great morning from her orient founts
Of silent fire, with wave on wave of light
And color, floods the earth and sky, and mounts
Through heights of pearly space, nor heeds, nor counts
Her triumphs, as she inundates the strands
Of continents, with joy and life on seas and lands;

II.

So shines our century, as the years unfold
The events and thoughts that claim the poet's lyre;
Not to lament a vanished age of gold,
But rather greet the time, whose broad sun-fire
Warms into life the world's supreme desire
Traced through the misty hollows of the night,
Half hid, but patient still to take the advancing light.

III.

Still art thou young, thou latest, loveliest age,
Thou fairest, healthiest daughter born of Time !
Might I but measure with my narrow gauge
Some fragment of thy height, fain would my rhyme
Stray through thy sunlit mountain-paths, and climb
To see the falsehoods of the centuries gone
Troop to their graves like ghosts, while thou exultest on !

IV.

O, broad and warm o'er hill and seagirt isle,
Thy morning splendors still illume the sky !
The hoary cliffs, the pines and cedars, smile
With rosy flushes.   Happy valleys lie
Long-shadowed.   Domes and steeples catch thine eye,
And smoke upcurls, and windows flash afar
O'er dew-wet meadow-farms, each town a golden star.

V.

Thou shinest over fields of waving grain,
And open barns, and tottering harvest-carts ;
O'er long-drawn iron track and flying train ;
O'er roar of steamers and of crowded marts ;
O'er clear-lit halls of sciences and arts ;
Where factory-maidens tend the whirling spool;
Or where small voices hum in the hushed village school.

VI.

Thy presence breathes, an influence calm and pure,
Here, where these interlacing elms surround
The walls our fathers founded to insure
The culture of the States ; a hallowed ground,
Through whose green academic shades resound
The echoing footsteps of two hundred years ;
And memory linked with hope instructs, inspires, and
      cheers.

VII.

By school and printing-press and message-wire ;
By ringing anvil and by furnace-blast ;
By dragon steeds of iron, winged with fire ;
By flying ocean-shuttles weaving fast
The old and new, the present and the past ;
By strong telluric force; by skill and art,
The world responds to thee, through brain and throb-
      bing heart.

VIII.

The strength of all the past is thine ; the blood
Of countless years thy intellectual light ;
The races of the world thy tidal flood.
Thou rollest on with ceaseless waves of bright,
Resistless influence, turning wrong to right,
Error to truth, treason to loyal faith,
Despair to wingéd hope, creating life from death.

IX.

We scarce may count the triumphs thou hast won,
So wide the treasury where thy wealth is stored.
And though thy years have more than half-way run
In time's great sandglass, what thou yet dost hoard
For future use, who knows ?   What unexplored
And unimagined powers shall yet be born ;
What glorious sons of light, what daughters of the morn !

X.

Thine are the years when Man asserts his claims, —
The birthright ages have so long denied,
The primogeniture of rights and aims
That vitalize the races ; thine the tide
That floats Humanity's tost bark o'er wide
And dreary seas, full-sailed, with wealth untold
Of long-imprisoned hopes, — O, richer far than gold !

XI.

And thine the central throne whence Science turns
To test, with sceptre of eternal law,
Through space, through spirit, every ray that burns
In stars and star-like souls ; and finds no flaw,
No discord, as with joy and reverent awe
Crowning their toil, her patient servants climb
The illumined peaks to read the unfolding scrolls of time.

XII.

We turn to gaze with wonder at the ghosts
Whose glamour filled the ages that have flown :
The sway of priests and kings ; the embattled hosts
That burned a blooming land, or built a throne ;
The terrors of a church that sought to own
The souls it crushed ; the inhuman laws that sealed
The founts of love, and stained a nation's virgin shield ;

XIII.

The unmanly morals of a shameless stage ;
The pomp of servile courts ; the robber's fame ;
All false ideals of a faithless age ;
All pride of birth that mocked the people's claim ;
All superstitions, in whose withering flame
The faithful saint, the daring thinker gave
Their memories to all time, their bodies to the grave.

XIV.

And yet all centuries that have leafed and flowered
Have dropped for us their foliage and their seed ;
Each age, by all the ancestral ages dowered,
Must reap the wholesome grain, the poisonous weed,
Heir to the bloom and blight alike decreed,
Twin-born, the alternate play of will and fate,
That weaves the mystic web of all our mortal state.

XV.

How shall we build with those time-crusted stones,
Dropped from the ruined arches of the past?
How gather up the Old World's discordant tones
In symphonies of hope?   Or how recast
The creeds of darker centuries, and at last,
With faith as strong, develop, not invent,
A fresher heart and soul for our vast Continent?

XVI.

The task is still before us, well begun
By souls whose fame is our delight and pride.
How our strong pioneers have toiled, and won
A hemisphere from chaos; how defied
The imperial thunderbolts that far and wide
Strewed other worlds with wrecks, but harmless fell,
Quenched hissing on our seas, let History proudly tell.

XVII.

Our century bends to them with thanks and praise;
Nor less to those forefathers sad and stern,
Who left the poisoned air and godless ways
Of courts corrupt, in fresher lands to earn
The right to think.   What though we sometimes turn,
In newer lights, their acrid saintliness
To jest, — they sowed the grain whose harvest we possess.

XVIII.

Theirs was the rough and bitter rind which wrapped
The priceless kernel planted on our shore.
The perishable shell, once all too apt
To style itself divine, survives no more.
The germ that in its stony nut it bore
Has sent abroad a thousand thriving shoots,
And filled our fields with trees, our homes with whole-
  some fruits.

XIX.

What though no Grecian and no Gothic thought
Of beauty grew to column, dome, or spire;
No artist's hand on stone or canvas wrought
Their heroes, saints, or nymphs; no lyric fire,
No music panting with divine desire,
In their plain Saxon lives expression found, —
They guarded the deep springs whose rills enrich our ground.

XX.

Within their theologic crypts they fed
The sacred fire that centuries have preserved;
The sanctities of home; the wholesome dread
Of lawless force; the trust that never swerved
In Providence divine; the faith that nerved
Their souls to found in freedom, knowledge, right,
A Commonwealth beyond the priest's or tyrant's blight;

XXI.

That common conscience which to-day divides
The right and wrong, and scorns to compromise
'Twixt Lucifer and God, — which so decides
For even-weighted justice, that no lies
Of false, fair-spoken sophists can surprise
Its steady vision and its honest aim,
Or tempt to pluck the fruit that breeds a nation's shame;

XXII.

That fearless love of truth which scorns the bait
Of party, sect, or clan; the open eye
And judgment, that can well afford to wait
The verdict of the future, can descry
Storms in the treacherous softness of the sky,
And through the windy watches of a night
Of tempest, note the path of sure-returning light;

XXIII.

That sweet humanity which feels that all
Who bear the name of woman and of man
Are one, — that none can languish, none can fall,
But somehow *all* must suffer from a ban
That darkens o'er the universal plan,
Yet strong as fate to oppose all force insane,
When mad rebellion roars to rend the state in twain; —

XXIV.

Such were the fruits whose seeds those Pilgrims brought
From far, o'er leagues of stormy winter brine.
And, as that ship which bore the Argonaut
Was set among the stars, and held divine,
So shall our classic Mayflower bloom and shine
Above a new-found Continent, with hope
That dims its earlier dream and clouded horoscope.

XXV.

For dark and chill, America, the years
That saw thee clinging like a drifting waif
To rocks and barren shores, thy hopes and fears
Rising and sinking like thy tides, till, safe
And self-reliant, vainly did they chafe
Against thee, though thy doors beyond the sea
Were shut against their child and deaf to freedom's plea.

XXVI.

Young Titan of the West! thy cradle swung
In storms. The wild winds were thy lullabies.
The cold contempt of kings around thee clung,
And gilded courtiers mocked thy infant cries;
Till, stronger grown, thee as their lawful prize
When they had roughly grasped, too late they learned
To fear the freeborn strength their parliaments had spurned.

XXVII.

But thou, for all their curses, gavest back
From battle-fields and councils, and the birth
Of free emprise, a light that cheered the black
Despair of millions whom both heaven and earth
Dowered with a blight; and on the sand and dearth
Of distant nations shed reviving dew,
And stirred the Old World's heart with longings strange
  and new.

XXVIII.

Nor this alone. The refuge thou hast been
For all the oppressed, a home for all who pined.
For them thy unwalled towns, thy prairies green,
Thy woods and streams; a charter unconfined;
The freedom of the fresh, untrammelled mind; —
All that can raise the vile and cheer the poor
Is theirs who come to seek a dwelling on thy shore.

XXIX.

Thou knew'st Columbia's youth, O Mother Age, —
The struggling youth of her, thy youngest child,
Fated to brave the ready-handed rage
Of tyranny, till peace and plenty smiled.
Thine eyes beheld o'er lakes and forests wild
Her liberal sway, her culture broad and free,
Grow with her growing strength, till sea was linked to sea.

XXX.

Thou knew'st the unsifted errors of that youth, —
Each blind, misguided impulse, crude and strong;
Each lapse from grand, ideal heights of truth
And justice.   Thou hast known the long,
Dishonorable reign of force and wrong;
The struggles of the manhood of the time
Against the serpent-folds of compromise and crime;

XXXI.

Against that curse of bondage, in the mesh
Of whose unhallowed network rich and poor
Alike were snared; that cancer in the flesh
The blood of countless hearts alone could cure, —
The costly price of all that could insure
Freedom and strength and honor to the state, —
The duty scorned so long, the lesson learned so late.

XXXII.

The inhuman codes that chained the slave, and drowned
The prayers of freemen lifted in his cause;
The people's mad delusions, cheered and crowned;
The mob's brute anarchy, — the tiger claws
That tore to shreds the wise ancestral laws, —
Shall they not lie entombed where none may dare
Infect with their decay the nation's purer air?

XXXIII.

For thee, our Country, may the advancing age
Evolve a destiny more nobly vast
Than ever stained with blood the antique page
In blurred and lurid records of the past.
For thou the keys of treasure-chambers hast,
From older lands and darker times concealed ;
Their past shall yield thee tools, — thy future is thy field.

XXXIV.

So, — like a master bending o'er the strings
Of some grand instrument not yet in tune,
And tempering every chord until it rings
Harmonious as the woods and waves in June,
Or as the obedient tides beneath the moon, —
So bends the Century o'er this Western land,
And wooes its hidden soul with skilled and loving hand ;

XXXV.

And, blending with its forces, hath unsealed
The invisible currents of diviner powers.
Here Science spreads her wealth, a boundless field ;
Art, Learning, Culture, climb to fruits and flowers.
Time makes a thousand opening vistas ours ;
A thousand varied triumphs of the soul
Glow on the nation's path, and gild the historic scroll.

XXXVI.

Behind us, like a thunder-storm o'erpast,
The clouds of battle fade.   Peace smiles again :
The Northern winds have blown their trumpet-blast ;
The Southern homes are answering to the strain
In other tones than those when death and pain
Shrieked their dread harvest-song of war, and reaped
The ghastly fields where sheaves of life in blood were
      heaped.

XXXVII.

We stood amid the wrecks of fated schemes.
We stumbled over falsehood's shattered stones.
Mid ruined columns and mid smoking beams
We toiled with firmer faith, and hope that owns
A future in whose miracles the tones
Amphion waked to build his fabled walls
Ring with the Century's march where'er its footstep falls.

XXXVIII.

Yet good and evil from the older lands,
Mixed with our own, like mingled dross and gold,
Half shaped and half refined, are in our hands.
We wait the patient fingers that shall mould
The mass to strength and grace as yet untold
Amid the annals of republics past, —
The states that rose like suns to set in storms at last.

XXXIX.

As once the sculptor on his statue wrought,
Till form to beauty grew, — from marble still
To breathing flesh, affection, motion, thought, —
So thou, O Mother-Age, shalt thou not fill
The measure of thy prophecies, until
The nation's unresponsive life shall warm
And glow beneath thy touch, beyond the sensuous form;

XL.

Until the lands that stretch from east to west
Shall know the presence of a power beyond
All bribes or party-limits, — unexpressed,
Yet felt, — to which all noble souls respond, —
The touch and pressure of the girdling bond
Of conscience, that no flaw or stain degrade
The strong, symmetric limbs in youth and grace arrayed?

XLI.

Thy future, O my Country, none may know;
Yet all the looms of Time are weaving swift
Thy destined warp and woof.   Above, below,
The viewless threads forever change and shift,
The noiseless shuttles fly.   The overdrift
Of fate moves on like air around the globe,
And blends the hues of storm and sunshine in thy robe.

XLII.

'T is thine to guard the wisdom that of old
Gave Rome her strength and Greece her art and grace;
The wealth that dims all treasuries of gold,
All glare of camps and courts; whose lights displace
Imperial pomp and splendor, and efface
The blazoned memories of the kings whose fame
Is but a puff of dust returning whence it came.

XLIII. ·

The time may come, — or is it but a hope
Of poets and enthusiasts born to dream,
But never prophesy, save when they ope
Their mouths Cassandra-like, while visions gleam
On sleeping worlds, — pale arctic lights that stream
And point their ghostly fingers to the pole,
Where shine the central constellations of the soul, —

XLIV.

A better time, perchance not ours to see,
Or see as some mirage in desert sands,
When, like the mighty Californian tree
By centuries matured, the nation stands
Close-grained and knit in nature's vital bands, —
Each State a spreading branch of evergreen,
Close to the mother-trunk that towers aloft between; —

12

XLV.

Perchance some future not so far away,
　When all we earned in war in peace we keep;
　When wealth and power shall dull no finer ray
　Of holier orbs; when deep shall answer deep,
　Not as when once the nation from her sleep
　Of cheating dreams woke to the battle's clang,
But souls to souls, as when the stars of morning sang.

XLVI.

Then shall the scholar and the teacher know
　How fruitless learning is, which sows its seeds
　On hearts where no deep sympathies can grow,
　Caught from the prophet-souls, in words and deeds,
　That from beneath the strata of dead creeds
　Spring to the surface of the age, — the true
And universal faith, — though old, forever new.

XLVII.

Then party camps shall cease to be a mart
　Where politicians ply their sordid trade;
　Then lowly worth and skill shall bear their part
　In offices and councils; then, unswayed
　By thirst for spoils, the honest man shall aid
　The state without the enforcement of a rod
To sell his free-born vote, — to cringe to a leader's nod.

XLVIII.

Then in the nation's capitol no blush
Of shame shall tinge the brows of those who plight
The nation's word to truth ; no bribe shall hush
The voice of reason, and no conscience slight
The everlasting statute-book of right :
But they who for the people stand shall speak
The people's wiser moods, nor selfish guerdons seek.

XLIX.

Then he who rules shall serve the country's cause,
Nor bow his knightly crest when factions roar,
Nor waver in the breath of fitful flaws
Blown by his friends or foes ; sound to the core
His heart of hearts, — though oft with travail sore
Perplexed and worn, still faithful at his post,
Waiting the grand results, though counting all the cost.

L.

Two such we knew, when mad rebellion gashed
The nation's limbs.   One, helmsman on the bark
Of state, when thunders roared and lightnings flashed,
Steered us to port, — himself the assassin's mark ;
The other, in whose breast no less the spark
Of honor shone, your Bay State raised to bless,
To govern, and to guide through years of anxious stress.

LI.

Another too, — late fallen, — who in the van
For years amid contending forces stood
A fearless champion of the rights of man;
Who dared and suffered, as he stemmed the flood,
By storms assailed, by flattering ripples wooed; —
The statesman, scholar, sage.   Let Harvard claim
His youth, your State his birth, the land his manhood's
        fame.

LII.

The great, the good, — the living and the dead,
Who wrought their earnest lives into the grain
And texture of the age; the hearts that bled;
The brains that toiled for truth, not power or gain, —
These are the saviors of the race.   In vain
The historian writes, in vain the poet sings,
Who knows not, as they pass, the time's anointed kings!

LIII.

Like glowing pictures in some missal old
Whose dulled and yellowed leaves in dust were laid,
The illumined pages start to life.   Behold
The noble men and women who have made
The light of memories that can never fade;
The aroma of all history, — the bloom
And spice of time, — though dead, still fragrant in the
        tomb.

LIV.

Such is the life the nation craves.   For such
No toil, no aspiration can we waste.
O land of hope and promise! let no touch
Of that Promethean fire whose flame effaced
The gods of darkness pass unfelt, no taste
Of baser glory lure thee from the streams
Whose crystal springs are hid in thy prophetic dreams.

LV.

And as along thy darkening ocean strand
Thy Pharos-towers their punctual stars illume
At eventide ; and ships from every land
Shun, toiling through the waves, the sailor's doom, —
So turn thy living lamps upon the gloom
Of storm-tost nations, that thy constant rays
May bless the world, and prove thy crowning fame and
        praise !

THE LAY OF THRYM; OR, THE HAMMER RECOVERED.

A VERSIFICATION FROM THE OLD NORSE EDDA OF SÆMUND
THE LEARNED.

WROTH was Vingthor when awaking he his mighty
    hammer missed,
Felt about him, shook his beard, and smote his forehead
    with his fist.
"Hear, O Loki, what I tell thee, known to none above,
    below;
Stolen is the Æsir hammer.   Swift to Freyia let us go."
To the dwelling of fair Freyia straight they flew as swift
    as wind.
"Lend thy feather-dress, O Freyia; I my hammer fain
    would find."

"Though 't were woven gold or silver, I would lend it,"
    Freyia said.
Then with whistling plumage Loki over plains and moun-
    tains sped.

Flew beyond the Æsirs' dwellings, till he came to Jötun-
lands.

On a mound sat Thrym, the Lord of Thursar, plaiting
golden bands,

Plaiting collars for his greyhounds, smoothing down his
horses' manes.

" Why to Jötunheim alone, O Loki, com'st thou o'er the
plains ? "

" Hast thou hidden Vingthor's hammer? Ill betide
thee if thou hast ! "

" I have hidden Vingthor's hammer, in the earth full
many a rast ;

None shall get it thence again, though he should labor
all his life,

Till he brings to me fair Freyia for my own and wedded
wife."

Then with whistling plumage Loki flew beyond the
Jötunland

Till within the Æsirs' courts he saw the mighty Vingthor
stand.

" Thou hast labored ; hast thou prospered ? Tell thy
tidings from the air ;

They who sit are often false, although their speech be
smooth and fair."

" I have labored, I have prospered. Thrym thy hammer
   took, O king.
None shall get it thence save he who Freyia for his wife
   will bring."

Forth to Freyia then they flew, and first of all these
   words they said :
" Put thy bridal raiment on, O Freyia ; thou with Thrym
   must wed.
Ride with us to Jötunheim.   The Thursar's lord shall be
   thy spouse."
Then did Freyia chafe with anger, and she knit her
   queenly brows,
And the Æsirs' palace. trembled as she paced it through
   and through,
And the famed Brisinga necklace from her neck in shivers
   flew.

" I should be the frailest woman and the basest of my
   time,
If with thee, in bridal raiment, I should ride to Jötun-
   heim ! "

Straightway then in council gathered all the Æsir to
   debate
How Hlorridi's hidden hammer they should rescue from
   its fate.

Heimdall, then, of Æsir brightest, thus amid the gods
    did speak :
" Let Thor dress in bridal raiment, with the necklace on
    his neck ;
By his side the keys shall jingle, round his knees a gown
    be spread,
Jewels sparkle on his breast, a golden coif upon his head."

Then outspoke the mighty Vingthor, " Shall a woman's
    part be mine ?
For the gods will smile to see me robed in bridal raiment
    fine."

Then spake Loki, " Mighty Thor, such words do not
    become thee well :
If thy hammer thou shalt lose, in Asgard will the Jötuns
    dwell."

So in bridal robes they dressed him ; like a maiden he
    was led.
By his side the keys did jingle, round his knees a gown
    was spread,
Jewels sparkled on his breast, a golden coif upon his
    head.

12 *   R

Then said Loki, " I will aid thee, as thy servant for a
    time,
And we two will ride together till we come to Jötun-
    heim."

Swift the goats were caught and harnessed ; swift and far
    their feet did run.
Rocks were shivered, earth ablaze. To Jötunheim rode
    Odin's son.

Thrym, the Lord of Thursar, shouted : " Up now, every
    Jötun's son ;
Freyia for my wife they bring me, — Niord's maid from
    Noatun.
Hither bring the gold-horned cattle, — oxen black, the
    Jötun's pride.
Treasures I have many ; only needed Freyia for my bride."

In the evening came the Jötuns. Beer for them was
    brought in pails.
Thor alone devoured an ox, and salmons eight with bones
    and scales.
All the sweetmeats women fancy disappeared with won-
    drous speed,
While he quenched his thirst by drinking three huge
    horns of foaming mead.

Then said Thrym, the Lord of Thursar, " Never in my
  life I saw
Maidens drink such draughts of mead, or brides with
  such a hungry maw ! "
Said the crafty Loki, sitting as a handmaid all this time,
" Eight nights Freyia naught has eaten, longing so for
  Jötunheim."

'Neath her veil Thrym stooped to kiss her, but sprang
  back along the hall ; —
" Why are Freyia's eyes so piercing ? — Sparks of fire my
  heart appall ! "
Said the crafty Loki, sitting as a handmaid all the time,
" Eight nights Freyia has not slept, so eager she for
  Jötunheim."

In then came the Jötun's sister ; for a bride-gift dared to
  crave.
" Give me all thy ruddy rings, if thou my love wouldst
  seek to have."

" Bring the hammer now ! " Thrym shouted. " Let us
  consecrate the bride.
Lay Miöllner on her knee ; naught can now our lives
  divide."

In his breast then laughed Hlorridi, when his hammer he
    beheld.

Up he rose and slew the Jötuns, — all the Jotun race he
    felled ;

Felled the Jötun's aged sister, who a bride-gift sought to
    gain, —

She, instead of golden rings, by Vingthor's hammer-stroke
    was slain.

So got Odin's son his hammer from the Jotuns back
    again.

MICHAEL ANGELO BUONAROTTI.

Read at a Celebration of the Four Hundredth Anniversary of his Birth, by the New England Women's Club, Boston, March 6, 1875.

I.

THIS is the rugged face
Of him who won a place
　　Above all kings and lords;
Whose various skill and power
Left Italy a dower
No numbers can compute, no tongue translate in words.

II.

Patient to train and school
His genius to the rule
　　Art's sternest laws required;
Yet, by no custom chained,
His daring hand disdained
The academic forms by tamer souls admired.

III.

In his interior light
Awoke those shapes of might,
   Once known, that never die;
Forms of Titanic birth,
The elder brood of earth,
That fill the mind more grandly than they charm the eye.

IV.

Yet when the master chose,
Ideal graces rose
   Like flowers on gnarléd boughs;
For he was nursed and fed
At Beauty's fountain-head,
And to the goddess pledged his earliest, warmest vows.

V.

Entranced in thoughts whose vast
Imaginations passed
   Into his facile hand,
By adverse fate unfoiled,
Through long, long years he toiled;
Undimmed the eyes that saw, unworn the brain that
      planned.

VI.

A soul the Church's bars,
The State's disastrous wars
    Kept closer to his youth.
Though rough the winds and sharp,
They could not bend or warp
His soul's ideal forms of beauty and of truth.

VII.

Like some cathedral spire
That takes the earliest fire
    Of morn, he towered sublime
O'er names and fames of mark
Whose lights to his were dark ;
Facing the east, he caught a glow beyond his time.

VIII.

Whether he drew, or sung,
Or wrought in stone, or hung
    The Pantheon in the air ;
Whether he gave to Rome
Her Sistine walls or dome,
Or laid the ponderous beams, or lightly wound the stair ;

IX.

Whether he planned defence
On Tuscan battlements,
   Fired with the patriot's zeal,
Where San Miniato's glow
Smiled down upon the foe,
Till Treason won the gates that mocked the invader's
      steel;

X.

Whether in lonely nights
With Poesy's delights
   He cheered his solitude;
In sculptured sonnets wrought
His firm and graceful thought,
Like marble altars in some dark and mystic wood, —

XI.

Still, proudly poised, he stepped
The way his vision swept,
   And scorned the narrower view.
He touched with glory all
That pope or cardinal,
With lower aims than his, allotted him to do.

XII.

A heaven of larger zone —
Not theirs, but his — was thrown
   O'er old and wonted themes.
The fires within his soul
Shone like an aureole
Around the prophets old and sibyls of his dreams.

XIII.

Thus self-contained and bold,
His glowing thoughts he told
   On canvas or on stone,
He needed not to seek
His themes from Jew or Greek;
His soul enlarged their forms, his style was all his own.

XIV.

Ennobled by his hand,
Florence and Rome shall stand
   Stamped with the signet-ring
He wore, where kings obeyed
The laws the artists made.
Art was his world, and he was Art's anointed king.

XV.

So stood this Angelo
Four hundred years ago ;
    So grandly still he stands,
Mid lesser worlds of Art,
Colossal and apart,
Like Memnon breathing songs across the desert sands.

ON RE-READING TENNYSON'S PRINCESS.

IF at this moment, in his distant isle
   And home, shut in by trees and ivied walls,
Where, hidden like the fountains of the Nile,
   He dreams among his palms and waterfalls, —
If there he knew how one beneath the pines
   Of Transatlantic lands, to him unknown,
Followed with glowing throb the poet's lines
   From page to page o'er all the waves of tone,
And read with stirring pulse and moistened eyes,
   And fancy in delighted tumult caught
Mid fairy splendors, visionary skies,
   And wild Æolian melodies of thought, —
Should then this stranger tell him all he felt,
   In speech, or letter burdened with his praise,
Think you that proud, sequestered soul would melt
   To answer from behind his British bays?
Nay, might he not his gates more closely bar

Against the intrusion, as of one that sought
With alien touch to unsphere the poet's star,
    And dwarf with diagrams his orbéd thought?

So have I whistled to a woodland thrush
    That charmed the silence of a forest green:
Sudden the liquid cadence ceased to gush;
    Deep in the leafy gloom he hid unseen.
And so the poet sings, nor can unmask
    With gloss of random talk his secret runes.
Hope not the English nightingale will task
    His tongue beneath the old, unbidden tunes.
Nor seek to snare the aroma of the rose
    That fills the garden with its mystic scents;
Nor, when the enchanted stream of music flows,
    Press a prose comment from the instruments.
Enough that one who prompts the melody
    Of younger bards and lords it in their style
Should sing unanswered, where alone and free
    He dreams amid his fountains of the Nile.

SONNETS.

THE HIGHER LAW.

MAN was not made for forms, but forms for man.
And there are times when law itself must bend
To that clear spirit always in the van,
Outspeeding human justice. In the end
Potentates, not humanity, must fall.
Water will find its level, fire will burn,
The winds must blow around the earthly ball,
The earthly ball by day and night must turn;
Freedom is typed in every element.
Man must be free, if not through law, why then
Above the law, until its force be spent,
And justice brings a better. But, O, when,
Father of Light, when shall the reckoning come
To lift the weak, and strike the oppressor dumb?

    1850.

CIRCUMSTANCE.

THERE are dark spots on yonder mountain-side,
So black that they seem fixed and rooted there :
But they will not, believe me, long abide ;
The clouds that cast them vanish into air.
So are there mountain minds who sometimes dare
Lift to the world their seeming blemishes,
Shadows of circumstance.   Do not compare
These with the vices the eye daily sees,
Blighting the bloom of spirits tamely hedged
In the unwholesome swamps that sleep below,
Where the malaria of accepted lies
Thins the dull blood to meagre virtues pledged.
Better endure the clouds that come and go,
Than court the infected shades where freedom dies.

SHAKESPEARE.

It needs no bow o'erstrained to wing the shaft
Of wit and wisdom. When great poets sing,
Into the night new constellations spring,
With music in the air that dulls the craft
Of rhetoric. So when Shakespeare sang or laughed,
The world with long, sweet Alpine echoes thrilled,
Voiceless to scholars' tongues no muse had filled
With melody divine. Athirst, men quaffed
His airy, electric words like heavenly wine.
The mountain summits of that Orient land
Outsoar the level of our praises fine.
All others lie around like hills of sand,
With here and there a green isle or a palm,
That whispers pleasantly when days are calm.

THE GARDEN.

NAUGHT know we but the heart of summer here.
On the tree-shadowed velvet lawn I lie,
And dream up through the close leaves to the sky,
And weave Arcadian visions in a sphere
Of peace.   The steaming heat broods all around,
But ònly lends a quiet to the hours.
The aromatic life of countless flowers,
The singing of a hundred birds, the sound
Of rustling leaves, go pulsing through the green
Of opening vistas in the garden walks.
Dear Summer, on thy balmy breast I lean,
And care not how the moralist toils or talks;
Repose and Beauty preach a gospel too,
Deep as that sterner creed the Apostles knew.

THE GARDEN (CONTINUED).

Is there no praise of God amid the bowers
Of summer idleness?   Still must we toil
And think, and tease the conscience, and so soil
With over-careful fingering the flowers
That blow within the garden of the heart?
Still must we be machines for grinding out
Thin prayers and moralisms?   Much I doubt,
Pale priest of a thorn-girded church, thy part
Is small in this wide breathing universe.
Least can I find thy title and thy worth
Here, where with myriad chords the musical earth
Is rhyming to the enraptured poet's verse.
Better thy cowl befits thy cloister's gloom;
Its shadow blots the garden and its bloom.

1852.

TO G. W. C.

GIORGIONE MIO! In your brilliant books,
Spiced through with odors from the balmy East,
And musical as winds and woodland brooks,
Pages for fragrance as for solid feast,
You have touched sweetly on a few bright days
Under the blue dome·of Italia's sky,
When side by side we drank the golden haze
Whose wondrous light from us can never die;
And sweetly, covertly, you twined my name
In the rich wreath you flung before the world.
Dear Friend! for you I fain would do the same;
And when this small bouquet that I have twirled
Upon the stage where you are gathering fame,
Catches your eye, you 'll know from whom it came.

1853.

TO W. W. S.

—◆—

I DID not think to sail with you, dear friend,
Over the waters of this charméd bay,
And bring you to my summer home, to spend
Together such a sweet and sunny day.
As we sped on, a shadowy fear there lay
Half o'er my hope, that accident might scrawl
The new-turned leaf in this fair book of May.
But thanks to the kind powers, I tasted all
For which I longed ; and in these grape-vine bowers
Upon the terrace by the sea, I felt
All harmonies of nature blend with ours,
And in the fleeting moments calmly melt,
While yon blue waves and purple mountain stood
Wrapt in the soft light of our genial mood.

SORRENTO, ITALY, May, 1848.

TO W. W. S.

———

So many years have passed, so far away
You seem, since arm in arm and eye to eye
We talked together, while the great blue sky
Of Rome smiled over us day after day,
Or on the flower-starred villa grounds we lay
Beneath the pines, while poesy and art
And mirth lent us one common mind and heart.
So long ago ! while we are growing gray,
And neither knows the life the other leads,
Shut in our separate spheres of thought and change.
Friend of my youth, how oft my spirit needs
The old, responsive voice !   Silence is strange,
That so cónspires with Time.   O, let us break
The spell, and speak, at least for old love's sake !

New York, April 9, 1870.

TO O. B. F.

To you, rejected by the church which most
Vaunts its own outgrowth from the older creeds,
Yet, jealous of God's boundless Pentecost,
Disowns all plants from its own flying seeds,
And props its stalk on formulas and texts,
Close shut from blowing winds of freer thought, —
To you, O friend, we turn, who, leaving sects
And rites outworn, have ever bravely sought
To find and lead the way to ampler heights
Of vision and of faith.   Your voice we hear,
Rich with the earnest eloquence of truth ;
And, following where its cheering tone invites,
The fogs of doubt disperse, the sky is clear,
And the wide prospect smiles with hope and youth.

TO O. B. F. (CONTINUED).

ALONE you stand, a herald of the morn
Of reason, faith, and large humanity, —
Auroral airs of earth and heaven born,
Blown from the east across time's changeful sea.
One day the world will know you, ranked with those
Who foremost in the nation's honor stand, —
The poet seers, who, as the century grows,
Give it a shape, with heart and brain and hand
Pledged to the truth.   I only say what all
Will know, when clearer lamps are lit than now
In Christendom's dim crypts stand flickering low ;
And fain to you would bring some coronal
Worthier than this small wreath of song I weave :
The fuller praise the riper times will give.

1870.

YOUTH AND AGE.

WHEN young, I slighted art, yet sighed for fame;
Dashed into careless rhyme, and toyed with thought.
When art and thoughts with age and wisdom came,
I laid aside the verse that youth had wrought.
These fruits, I said, were green, that from my bough,
When windy fancies swept, so lightly fell;
A mellower autumn sun is shining now,
That shames the cruder crop once loved so well.
Yet when it chanced some tender hearts had found
A sweeter flavor in the juiceless things
That lay in heaps neglected on the ground,
Than in the fruits the ripening season brings,
I thought, Must life retrace its pilgrimage,
And youth sing songs for youth, and age for age?

1874.

POEMS OF THE WAR.

THE BURIAL OF THE FLAG.

AN INCIDENT IN MEMPHIS, TENNESSEE, 1861.

O, WHO are these that troop along, and whither do they
  go?
Why move they thus with measured tread, while funeral
  trumpets blow?
Why gather round that open grave in mockery of woe?

They stand together on the brink, they shovel in the
  clod;
But what is that they bury deep? Why trample they the
  sod?
Why hurry they so fast away, without a prayer to God?

It was no corpse of friend or foe. I see a flag uprolled;
The golden stars, the gleaming stripes, are gathered fold
  on fold,
And lowered into the hollow grave, to rot beneath the
  mould.

Then up they hoisted all around, on towers and hills and
　　crags,
The emblems of their traitorous schemes, their base dis-
　　union flags.
That very night there blew a wind that tore them all to
　　rags !

And one that flaunted bravest by the storm was swept
　　away,
And hurled upon the grave in which our country's banner
　　lay,
Where, soaked with rain and stained with mud, they found
　　it the next day.

From out the North a power comes forth, — a patient
　　power too long, —
The spirit of the great, free air, — a tempest swift and
　　strong ;
The living burial of our flag, it will not brook that wrong.

The stars of heaven shall gild her still; her stripes like
　　rainbows gleam ;
Her billowy folds like surging clouds o'er North and
　　South shall stream.
She is not dead, she lifts her head, she takes the morn-
　　ing's beam !

The banner of the unsevered States, — though buried in
    the dust,
She is not dead; she springs to life; her cause, like
    truth's, is just;
She leads the van, her meteor flame directs the thunder-
    gust!

That storm of lightning, wind, and rain shall sweep the
    country clean,
Till sweet airs breathe, and bright suns shine the cloudy
    rifts between,
And all the vales shall bloom anew, and all the hills be
    green!

June 4, 1861.

THE ROSE OF DEATH.

A BALLAD OF THE WAR.

I.

"SHE told me of a rose
In a Southern field that grows;
But my love, my love, — she little knows
  The flower that I may bring.
In the heart of the perilous storm,
By the roads where our foemen swarm,
In the fields of death it blossoms warm;
  But on I march, and sing
      O the red, red rose,
      She little knows
      The flower that I may bring!

II.

" For I am Northern born:
She, — only yestermorn
I saw on her lips her Southern scorn.
  Coldly she saw me fling

My student's cap away;
Coldly she heard me say,
' In the Union ranks I march to-day ! '
    And here I march, and sing ; —
        O the red, red rose,
        She little knows
        The flower that I may bring !

III.

" Ah, it were sweet to know,
When face to face with the foe,
That a loving heart did with me go,
    Like the kiss of a talisman ring,
Praying that death might spare
The life of her lover there,
In the cannon's smoke and the trumpet's blare.
    No matter.   I march, and sing
        O the red, red rose,
        She little knows
        The flower that I may bring !

IV.

" Her love, — have I lost it all,
Because at my country's call
I said, ' 'T were better in battle to fall
    Than see this treason cling ! '

T

Her friends are my foemen now,
' Traitor ' is writ on each brow.
On, comrades! I have made a vow,
    And I breathe it as I sing
       O the red, red rose,
       She little knows
       The flower that I may bring ! "

v.

Deep in the battle there
His breast to the guns is bare,
Where flame and smoke befoul the air,
    Swords clash and rifles ring.
" She loves," he cried, " but the brave
Who fight for the chains of the slave.
What then ?   I can fill a patriot's grave,
    Though she may jest, and sing
       O the red, red rose,
       He thinks that he knows
       The flower he home will bring ! "

vi.

All terror the soldier scorns,
Mid the cannon and clanging horns;
From the bristling fields of the bayonet thorns
    A rose on his breast he will bring.

What is it?   A death-shot red
To his fearless heart has sped;
With his face to the fire, he reels, — he is dead!
   And the soldiers who bear him sing
      O the blood-red rose !
      She little knows
      The flower that home we bring !

VII.

Ah, sad were the streets the morn
When that brave form was borne,
Wrapped in the Union banner, torn
   Like a wounded eagle's wing.
At her window the maiden stood,
Changed from her angry mood;
And she saw on her lover's breast the blood;
   And the death-march seemed to sing
      O the blood-red rose
      From our country's foes
      Is the only flower we bring !

VIII.

She rushed to the bier with a cry.
" O God ! " she said, " it was I
Who sent him, without one kiss, to die
   In the flush of his morn of spring !

Too late, — this pang at my breast!
Ah, let me at least go rest
In the grave where you bear the dearest, best!
  And the pitying winds shall sing
    Here Love's red rose
    Met Death's, at the close
    Of their lives, in eternal spring!"

NOVEMBER 8TH, 1864.

——◉——

JOY to our reunited States! — one struggle more has
    passed.
A load is lifted from our hearts. The traitors stand
    aghast.
The Nation writes its record clear; — our land is saved at
    last!

Calmly mid armed conspirators this day a work is done,
Amid the thunder of the war one bloodless field is won,
That on the page of history glows in letters like the sun.

One effort of the people towards the source of primal light;
One forward leap across the gulf from chaos and from
            night;
One stride along the century to union based on right!

We see the rainbow span the gloom. We hear the deep-
toned bell
That strikes the nation's hour of noon, toll slavery's
funeral-knell.
Rebellion totters to its doom. The watchman cries,
" All 's well."

Not as a party's triumph-shout rings out this people's
voice.
When Life and Death are in the scales, who wavers in
his choice ?
O flower of nations, blighted now no more, rejoice, re-
joice !

O morning-glory of the earth ! thy garden in the west
Is wet once more with falling dews of peace and love and
rest.
Thou liftest up thy drooping head. All, all is for the
best !

Thy petals are the sister States. Though scorched by
battle's fire,
Not one shall wither in the blast, now hot with foemen's
ire ;
But fairer yet thy leaves shall rise, and broader still and
higher.

No stain upon thy radiant disk, thy colors all re-blent,
Washed in the thunder-storm of war, to thee that storm
      has lent
Strength for the future that o'erpays the blood thy roots
      have spent.

My country, in this hour of hope, O, send to those who
      bear
The burden of the war to-day our help, our strength, our
      prayer ;
Our greeting of the coming day, our farewell to despair !

O soldiers of a thousand fields !   O brothers strong and
      young !
Brave hearts who breast the battery fires, — heroes un-
      known, unsung, —
Long galaxies of starlike lives and deaths above us hung !

What record of the historian's pen, what poet's loftiest
      lays,
What parallel from out the grand and stern old Roman
      days,
What sculptured monument those lives, those deaths, can
      overpraise !

We slumber calmly in our beds, and by our firesides read
The story of your battles grim.   We see you march and
      bleed;
From hospital and prison hear your cries of pain and
      need.

Ye march that we may rest, our land free from the slave-
      lord's rod;
Ye fall, that juster laws may flower from out your blood-
      stained sod;
Ye die, that we may live a life more true to man and God.

Through drenching rains and scorching fires we see you
      fighting still, —
No rest by day, no sleep by night, no joy your cup to fill, —
While we step calmly to the polls to vote the nation's will.

A little sprinkling of the rain while standing in the
      queue,
We wait our turn amid the crowd to see our ballot through,
Then homeward wend, and thank our stars we 've served
      our country too.

A little round of speech-making mid captivated ears;
A few intense mass-meetings, a few huzzas and cheers;
Some sleepless nights, some busy days, some weeks of
      hopes and fears; —

Such are the battles that we fight here in our peaceful
    North.
One hour of life in camp and field whole days of this
    seems worth;
Yet none the less is victory won.   The nation's will goes
    forth,

Once and forever forth, — the arm is held that beat it
    back; —
Goes forth to unmask the traitor's plots, hunts on the
    foeman's track;
Stands like the rock against the sea, the sun mid tempest's
    wrack.

From east to west it thrills and rings, and tells this lesson
    plain:
Self-government henceforth achieved, our seeming losses
    gain;
War leads to peace, and yet no peace till slavery's life be
    slain.

O strange and wondrous Providence, that sealed the peo-
    ple's eyes,
Lest all too soon these mighty truths within their creed
    should rise!
We fought amid the clouds at first, — how slowly we grow
    wise!

14

Those truths we scorned four years ago now on our
    banners glow,
Burnt in and branded on our souls, in battling with the
    foe;
Ay, worn as amulets to shield our fame where'er we go.

We praise that stern fanatic, to death and triumph gone;
That voice crying in the wilderness, — rough herald of
    the dawn.
Our John the Baptist is not dead; his soul is marching
    on!

We cancel creeds of former days.   Our timid codes are
    null.
We leave our ancient council-fires to smoulder low and
    dull.
We trust the nation's newer life will heap its measure full.

A breeze of morning sweeps the sky.   Old errors one by
    one
Are crowded back upon the south, a cloud-bank dark and
    dun,
Or hang in air like floating mists beneath the rising sun.

But still the northern winds must blow; yes, still war's
    bitter blast

Must purify that poisoned air, till, force by right surpassed,
Each groaning bondsman breaks his chains, and all are
    free at last.

No half-truth now! Our feet are set upon a higher
    ground;
No more mid dawn's uncertain shades, by old delùsions
    bound;
The sun that shone on peaks alone now fills the vales
    around.

O trumpet voices of the press! O bards by visions
    stirred!
O leaders of the people's will! O preachers of the Word!
Yours be the freest, truest tones the nation yet has heard!

Sound the keynote the age demands, — Humanity's great
    prayer;
A sigh for peace, but not a lull of foul and stagnant air,
A sleep on a volcano's brink, a stillness of despair:

No, not that helpless apathy, that torpor of the life
Drunk with the chloroform of lies, — the amputator's knife
Ready by one fell cut to end the giant nation's strife.

O bleeding land! thy North and South forever have
    been wed.

No quack shall drug thy cup, though bitter be the draught
    and red;

No knife shall touch thy limbs.   I see, I see thee lift thy
    head; —

I see thee smile with sad, stern eyes, triumphant o'er thy
    woes;

Strength that o'ertops the surgeon's skill through all thy
    members flows;

Thou standest as thou stoodst of old, a terror to thy foes.

I have no prophet's sight or speech, and yet I see thy
    form

Looming above the battle-smoke, unscathed amid the
    storm;

Around thy head the skies are blue, the sunshine still
    and warm.

Peaceful and wise I see thee sit, earth's youngest, fairest
    queen;

War's blackened wastes by freemen tilled, all waving gold
    and green;

From North to South, from sea to sea, no slave or tyrant
    seen;

Redeemed and strong forever. On field and hill and
town,
All prophet dreams shall be fulfilled in wisdom and
renown;
Thy newer life shall now begin, thy sun no more go
down!

SONNETS FOR THE TIMES.

APRIL, 1865.

I.

THE DARK TOWER.

"Childe Roland to the Dark Tower came."*   What
      then ?
The poet paints a mystery weird and dark,
Full of foreboding.   Bones and corpses stark,
On blighted moorland and in rotting fen,
Under the knight's adventurous feet protrude.
Voices like gusts of wind, warning and taunt,
Stun his bewildered ears.   The sunset slant
Shows the Black Tower against a sky of blood.
The hills like gloomy giants watch to see
His fall, as others fell.   He dauntless blows
His horn, and fights, and tells the tale.   So he
Who our grim tower of slavery overthrows
Shall well inspire our future minstrel's strain,
True son of knighthood, Roland come again.

* See Browning's poem.

II.

DELIVERANCE.

FOR never was a darker dungeon built
By king or pope in the old, wicked time, —
The lurid centuries when the lords of crime
Walked shameless in their robes of chartered guilt;
Churchman and statesman vying which could dye
With reddest ink of blood the historic page.
They played their part.   But our illumined age
Brooks not the insult, and flings back the lie,
When slave lords fight against the eternal tides,
When truth is twisted from its straight intent,
And freedom blighted in its loveliest spring.
The mask where hatred smiles and treachery hides
Is torn away at last.   The war-clouds bring
Deliverance from our long imprisonment.

III.

THE ABOLITIONISTS.

BRAVE men, far-sighted seers ! who on the rim
Of your high battlements looked clearly forth
Over the fog that stretched from south to north,
And callèd with warning voices down the dim
Blind valleys, " Men are children all of Him
Who made us all," — our cause for pride is slight,
That now so late we see the eternal Right
Shining like wings of heavenly seraphim.
True prophets, who discerned the cloud of war
Rise from the mist of long, delusive peace,
Pardon the eyes that could not pierce so far.
Long since the people's fears and doubtings cease ;
Our hands no longer in the darkness grope :
We share with you your toil, your faith, your hope.

IV.

THE DAWN OF PEACE.

FOUR years of war have driven afar the dream
Of union based on hollow compromise.
We wake to see the auroral splendors stream
Across the battle smoke from opening skies.
The demon, shrieking, tears us as he flies
Exorcised from our wrenched and bleeding frame.
O costly ransom! dearly purchased prize!
Release too long delayed! from sin and shame,
From evil compacts and from brutal laws,
Whose iron network all the land encaged.
Force never triumphed in a juster cause,
Nor bloody war was e'er so justly waged.
Henceforth our banner greets a cloudless morn.
Peace dawns at last.   The nation is re-born!

V.

THE DEATH-BLOW.

But yesterday the exulting nation's shout
Swelled on the breeze of victory through our streets;
But yesterday our gay flags flaunted out
Like flowers the south-wind wooes from their retreats, —
Flowers of the Union, blue and white and red,
Blooming on balcony and spire and mast,
Telling us that war's wintry storm had fled,
And spring was more than spring to us at last.
To-day, — the nation's heart lies crushed and weak;
Drooping and draped in black our banners stand.
Too stunned to cry revenge, we scarce may speak
The grief that chokes all utterance through the land.
God is in all.   With tears our eyes are dim,
Yet strive through darkness to look up to Him!

VI.

THE MARTYR.

No, not in vain he died, not all in vain, —
Our good, great President.   This people's hands
Are linked together in one mighty chain,
Knit tighter now in triple woven bands,
To crush the fiends in human mask, whose might
We suffer, O, too long !   No league or truce
Save *men* with *men*.   The devils we must fight
With fire.   God wills it in this deed.   This use
We draw from the most impious murder done
Since Calvary.   Rise, then, O countrymen !
Scatter these marsh-light hopes of union won
Through pardoning clemency.   Strike, strike again !
Draw closer round the foe a girdling flame !
We are stabbed whene'er we spare.   Strike, in God's
      name !

VII.

OUR COUNTRY.

As on some stately ship, with land in view,
The last sea-swell beneath her gliding keel,
Sudden, like God's hand clad in blinding steel,
A thunder-bolt falls crashing from the blue,
Shattering the mast, a sulphurous cloud rolls through
The sails and rigging, while with quivering lips
The sailors see the deck all strewn with chips
And shreds and splinters, yet make all ado
To mend their loss, and still the ship sails on :
So, reeling from the shock, our Ship of State
Repairs the chasm left by the fall of him
Who stood her mainmast : onward we have gone ;
Sound at the core, though tossed by storms but late,
Nearing our port, we cross the shadows dim.

Cambridge : Electrotyped and Printed by Welch, Bigelow, & Co.

The Romantic Tradition in American Literature

An Arno Press Collection

Alcott, A. Bronson, editor. **Conversations with Children on the Gospels.** Boston, 1836/1837. Two volumes in one.

Bartol, C[yrus] A. **Discourses on the Christian Spirit and Life.** 2nd edition. Boston, 1850.

Boker, George H[enry]. **Poems of the War.** Boston, 1864.

Brooks, Charles T. **Poems, Original and Translated.** Selected and edited by W. P. Andrews. Boston, 1885.

Brownell, Henry Howard. **War-Lyrics** and Other Poems. Boston, 1866.

Brownson, O[restes] A. **Essays and Reviews Chiefly on Theology, Politics, and Socialism.** New York, 1852.

Channing, [William] Ellery (The Younger). **Poems.** Boston, 1843.

Channing, [William] Ellery (The Younger). **Poems of Sixty-Five Years.** Edited by F. B. Sanborn. Philadelphia and Concord, 1902.

Chivers, Thomas Holley. **Eonchs of Ruby:** A Gift of Love. New York, 1851.

Chivers, Thomas Holley. **Virginalia;** or, Songs of My Summer Nights. (Reprinted from *Research Classics,* No. 2, 1942). Philadelphia, 1853.

Cooke, Philip Pendleton. **Froissart Ballads,** and Other Poems. Philadelphia, 1847.

Cranch, Christopher Pearse. **The Bird and the Bell,** with Other Poems. Boston, 1875.

[Dall], Caroline W. Healey, editor. **Margaret and Her Friends.** Boston, 1895.

[D'Arusmont], Frances Wright. **A Few Days in Athens.** Boston, 1850.

Everett, Edward. **Orations and Speeches,** on Various Occasions. Boston, 1836.

Holland, J[osiah] G[ilbert]. **The Marble Prophecy,** and Other Poems. New York, 1872.

Huntington, William Reed. **Sonnets and a Dream.** Jamaica, N. Y., 1899.

Jackson, Helen [Hunt]. **Poems.** Boston, 1892.

Miller, Joaquin (Cincinnatus Hiner Miller). **The Complete Poetical Works of Joaquin Miller.** San Francisco, 1897.

Parker, Theodore. **A Discourse of Matters Pertaining to Religion.** Boston, 1842.

Pinkney, Edward C. **Poems.** Baltimore, 1838.

Reed, Sampson. **Observations on the Growth of the Mind.** *Including,* **Genius** (Reprinted from *Aesthetic Papers,* Boston, 1849). 5th edition. Boston, 1859.

Sill, Edward Rowland. **The Poetical Works of Edward Rowland Sill.** Boston and New York, 1906.

Simms, William Gilmore. **Poems:** Descriptive, Dramatic, Legendary and Contemplative. New York, 1853. Two volumes in one.

Simms, William Gilmore, editor. **War Poetry of the South.** New York, 1866.

Stickney, Trumbull. **The Poems of Trumbull Stickney.** Boston and New York, 1905.

Timrod, Henry. **The Poems of Henry Timrod.** Edited by Paul H. Hayne. New York, 1873.

Trowbridge, John Townsend. **The Poetical Works of John Townsend Trowbridge.** Boston and New York, 1903.

Very, Jones. **Essays and Poems.** [Edited by R. W. Emerson]. Boston, 1839.

Very, Jones. **Poems and Essays.** Boston and New York, 1886.

White, Richard Grant, editor. **Poetry:** Lyrical, Narrative, and Satirical of the Civil War. New York, 1866.

Wilde, Richard Henry. **Hesperia:** A Poem. Edited by His Son (William Wilde). Boston, 1867.

Willis, Nathaniel Parker. **The Poems, Sacred, Passionate, and Humorous, of Nathaniel Parker Willis.** New York, 1868.